Private Passion, Public Promise

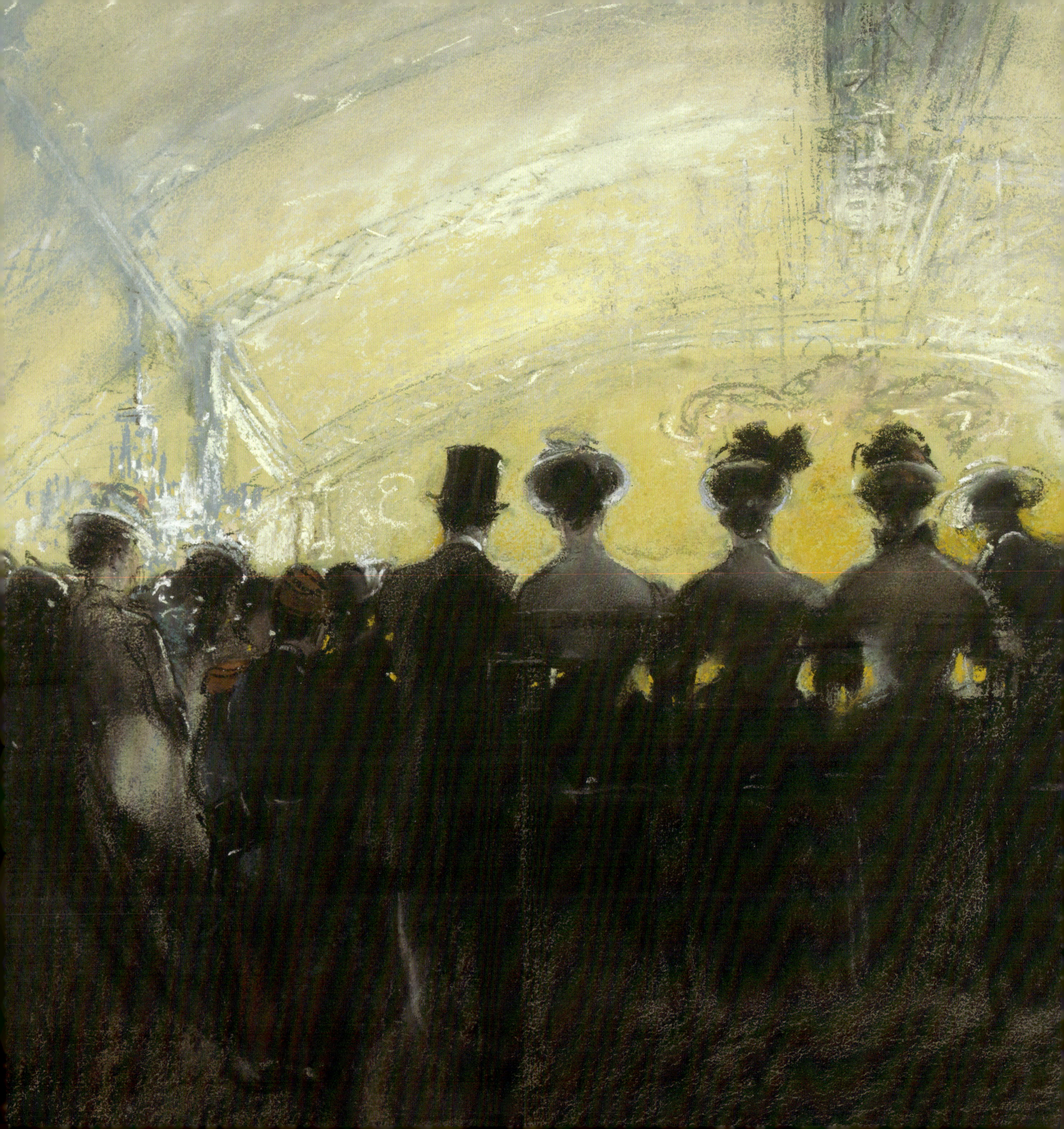

PRIVATE PASSION, PUBLIC PROMISE

The James W. and Frances G. McGlothlin Collection of American Art

Sylvia Yount

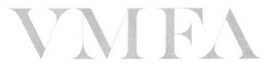

Virginia Museum of Fine Arts, Richmond

Distributed by The University of Virginia Press
Charlottesville and London

Library of Congress Cataloging-in-Publication Data

Virginia Museum of Fine Arts.

     Private passion, public promise : the James W. and Frances G. McGlothlin collection of American Art /

     Sylvia Yount.—1st ed.

     p.   cm.

     Includes index.

     ISBN 978-0-917046-95-7

1. Art, American—19th century—Exhibitions. 2. Art, American—20th century—Exhibitions.

3. McGlothlin, James W.—Art collections—Exhibitions. 4. McGlothlin, Frances G.—Art collections—Exhibitions.

5. Art—Virginia—Richmond—Exhibitions. 6. Virginia Museum of Fine Arts—Exhibitions.

I. Yount, Sylvia. II. Title. III. Title: James W. and Frances G. McGlothlin Collection of American Art.

     N6510.V57 2010

     709.73'074755451—dc22   2010002648

ISBN 978-0-917046-95-7

Produced by the Department of Publications, Virginia Museum of Fine Arts

200 N. Boulevard, Richmond, Virginia, 23220-4007 USA

Edited by Anne Adkins

Designed by Lauren Kitts

Photography by Katherine Wetzel and Travis Fullerton except page viii, michelsaborin.com; and
     page 3, Stephen Allen Photography.

Composed in Adobe InDesign with Garamond Premier Pro

Printed on Sappi McCoy Gloss by Worth Higgins & Associates, Richmond, Virginia

Cover: Robert Blum, *In the Laundry* (detail), 23; frontispiece: Everett Shinn, *Back Row, Folies-Bergère* (detail), 79;
chapter dividers: William Ranney, *Ice Gatherers* (detail), 4–5, 17; John Singer Sargent, *The Rialto* (detail), 18–19, 54;
George Bellows, *Summer City* (detail), 60–61, 64, 82; back cover: George Bellows, *Kids,* 63

Contents

Foreword

Three key elements define the art museum of today: the collection, the architectural space that frames the art, and the donors, trustees, staff, volunteers, and visitors who form the public face of our institutions. It is a rare synergy when all three elements coincide with happy and deliberate results as they have in the exhibition *Private Passion/Public Promise: The James W. and Frances G. McGlothlin Collection of American Art.* This showing of the McGlothlins's magnificent holdings of American art—among the leading private collections in this country—inaugurates the new McGlothlin Wing at the Virginia Museum of Fine Arts. Through their generosity and foresight, Jim and Fran McGlothlin have critically impacted the present and the future of the museum. In 2005, they offered both a gift of art and funding that then totaled $100 million; the collection's value has more than doubled today. With this magnanimous gift, Jim and Fran bestowed upon the museum a promised collection that captures the essence of mid-19th- to mid-20th-century American art.

Jim and Fran often regale me with stories of their pursuit and capture of compelling artworks. They collect with two purposes uppermost in mind: filling art historical gaps and complementing areas of established strength. Over time, they have refined their passion, carefully selecting works that fit perfectly into an already robust collection with its considerable strengths in late 19th-century and early 20th-century figurative painting, especially by John Singer Sargent, George Bellows, and other members of the Ashcan school. Incredibly, the McGlothlin collection meshes beautifully with the existing collection of American art at the Virginia Museum of Fine Arts—as if the two were always made for each other.

The alliterative title of this exhibition, *Private Passion/Public Promise,* is an ideal tribute to the McGlothlins. Passion typifies their collecting, and their promise to share their collection with Virginia and the world is something for which we are all eternally thankful.

Alex Nyerges
Director

vi

Acknowledgments

I first visited the Virginia Museum of Fine Arts in 2005, specifically to see the exhibition *Capturing Beauty: American Impressionist and Realist Paintings from the McGlothlin Collection,* curated by my predecessor David Park Curry. This impressive showing of some 30 masterworks of late 19th- and early 20th-century American art marked my initial encounter with a collection that I've come to greatly admire. Without question, the knowledge that these private holdings were destined for the Commonwealth's public museum influenced my subsequent decision to join VMFA's curatorial staff. Today, I am privileged to oversee an already choice array of American art—formed by talented colleagues and generous museum patrons over VMFA's 74-year history— that will be immeasurably enriched with the addition of the McGlothlins's gift.

It is a particular pleasure to showcase a broader swath of this private collection on the occasion of the opening of VMFA's new McGlothlin Wing and American art galleries. I'm grateful to all of my colleagues who have worked diligently to realize this collaborative effort, especially Lauren Kitts and Anne Adkins in Publications, Katherine Wetzel and Travis Fullerton in Photography, Mary Sullivan in Registration,

Tom Baker in Exhibition Design, and Elizabeth O'Leary in American Art. Outside of the museum, Chris Burke and Kate Lester deserve special recognition. My greatest thanks are extended to Jim and Fran McGlothlin for turning their "private passion" into a "public promise" that will benefit countless museum visitors in perpetuity. We are all in their debt.

Sylvia Yount
*Louise B. and J. Harwood Cochrane
Curator of American Art*

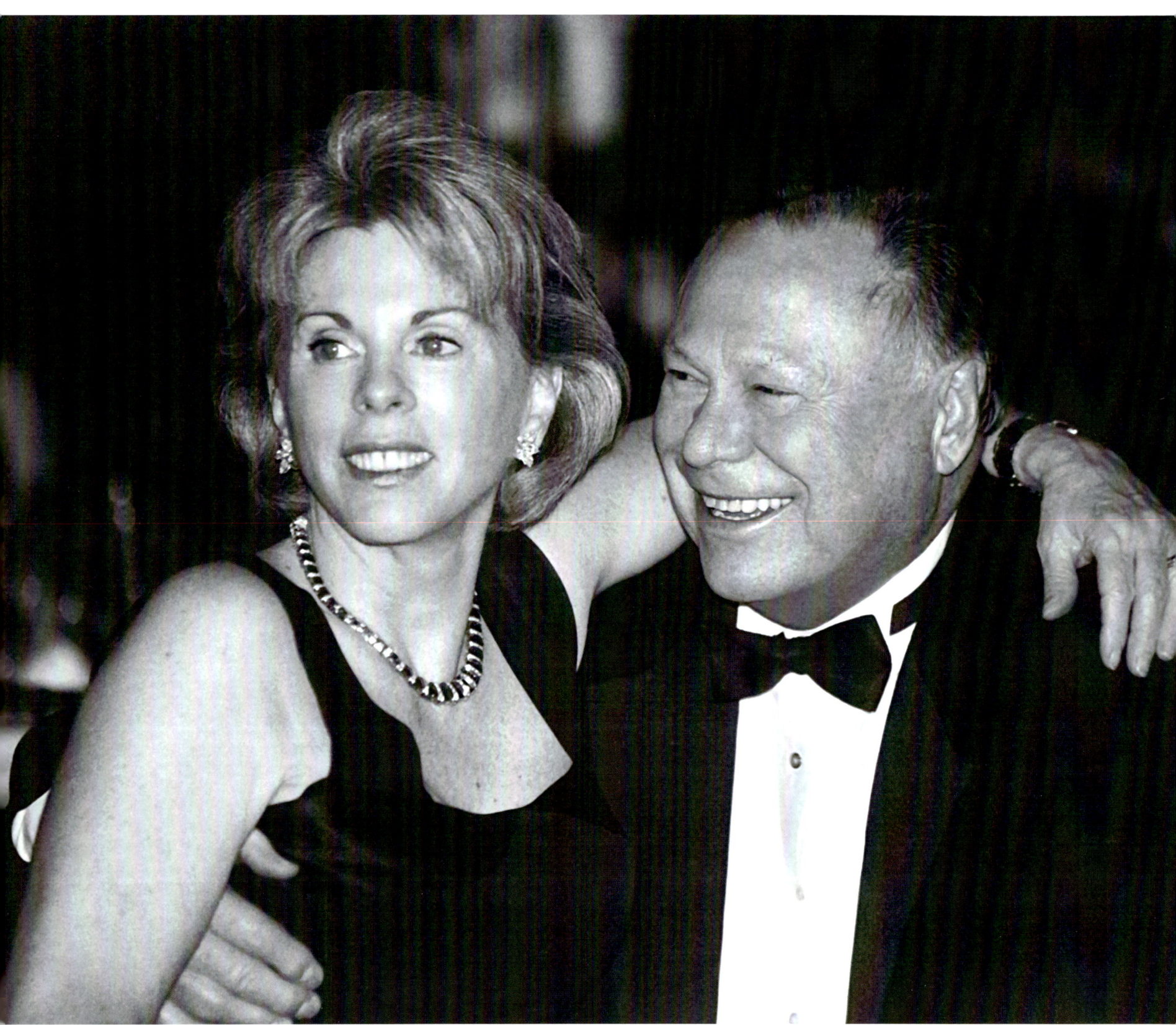

Frances G. and James W. McGlothlin

Interview

SYLVIA YOUNT: Jim and Fran, to my mind, you have built a very personal and distinctive collection by not pursuing "names," per se, but by focusing on the inherent strength of each work—that is, its technical competence, visual power, and aesthetic appeal. How did you embark on collecting and what was your initial motivation?

McGLOTHLINS: When we married, we wanted to find a mutual interest that we could enjoy well into old age. We've always focused on American art as we found it more challenging to collect because of its relative scarcity when compared with other types of cultural production. While we have a broader interest in America's past (we are native Virginians!), our primary focus is on the art's visual appeal rather than its history.

SY: Your collection features paintings, works on paper, and sculptures in that proportional order. Do you find you favor one medium over another?

McGLOTHLINS: We like both watercolors and oils, but collect these more for their individual qualities rather than to emphasize any one medium.

SY: The works featured in this exhibition range roughly from 1840 to 1925. Is there a particular time period, region, genre, or style that you find most compelling?

McGLOTHLINS: At this stage, we are especially drawn to works dating from the turn of the 20th century to the mid-1920s, as seen in the "Modern World" section of this exhibition and catalogue. That period was captured vividly by the Ashcan school, which holds particular interest. Our

very first acquisition was the striking 1924 oil, *Listening Boy,* by Robert Henri, the leader of this group of urban realists. And although we have collected widely in the intervening years, our most recent addition is George Luks's *The Hitch Team*—a beautiful and moving 1916 painting by Henri's friend and colleague.

SY: What first draws you to a work of art? Do you find you bring a more intuitive or studied approach to your appraisal?

McGLOTHLINS: Definitely an intuitive approach. And we're initially drawn to an object's subject matter far more than its style.

SY: How significant is provenance, that is, the work's ownership history? Do you see yourselves as part of a continuum of collectors?

McGLOTHLINS: While provenance is certainly significant, it's not our number-one priority. Our sense of ourselves as collectors is more in relation to our peers in the collecting community than to those who came before.

SY: How would you define your particular aesthetic or taste?

McGLOTHLINS: In addition to subject matter (we prefer a figural presence), the work's intrinsic beauty is paramount. We gravitate toward objects that allow you to apply your own subjective interpretations.

SY: When you first examine a work, do you consider its future home—for example, do you have a certain context, or setting, in mind when you're exploring an acquisition?

McGlothlins: No, not really; that thinking comes later, when we decide on where and how it will be displayed. We believe our objects live happily anywhere.

SY: Your collection has great strengths in a number of seminal American artists, for example, John Singer Sargent. What attracts you to his art, and can you describe the relationship between different Sargents in your holdings?

McGlothlins: We think John Singer Sargent had wide-ranging abilities, which we continue to discover as we live with a full variety of his pictures. The way his American and European subjects, rendered in oil and watercolor, speak to each other is remarkable. Collecting certain artists—George Bellows, Robert Blum, Childe Hassam, Robert Henri, Winslow Homer, Martin Johnson Heade, and George Luks, each in some depth—has always appealed to us. It's fascinating to see how their approach does (or doesn't) change in different works.

SY: What do you enjoy most about collecting?

McGlothlins: In the beginning, for Jim, it was mainly the chase and the "art" of the deal, but as our familiarity with American art deepened, it became intellectually challenging to further our knowledge about the artists and their chosen art forms. The relationships we've developed with other collectors have also been extremely rewarding.

SY: What advice would you give others interested in collecting American art? Do you find it's useful to seek the input of specialists, at least at the outset?

McGlothlins: We believe it is important to have academic advice regarding the quality of an object one intends to acquire as well as business advice from someone who is active in the market. These considerations led us at the beginning of our collecting to consult with Dr. Theodore Stebbins, curator of American art at the Harvard University Art Museums (and formerly at the Museum of Fine Arts, Boston), and Michael Altman, a New York dealer. Their advice and friendship have been invaluable over the years.

SY: Did you start with a goal to build a museum-worthy collection? When and why did you decide to make the Virginia Museum of Fine Arts a beneficiary?

McGlothlins: We began collecting for our own personal pleasure, and we've been fortunate to be able to live with these works, yet as our collection grew we started to feel a responsibility. Since we are Virginians by birth and love VMFA, ultimately giving them to the Commonwealth was a natural and easy choice.

SY: How do you envision your collection developing in the future?

McGlothlins: We are always looking to raise the quality of our collection and now also keep in mind how a particular piece would mesh with the museum's American holdings. It's a mutually beneficial and auspicious collaboration as seen by the simultaneous opening of this special exhibition and VMFA's newly expanded American art galleries.

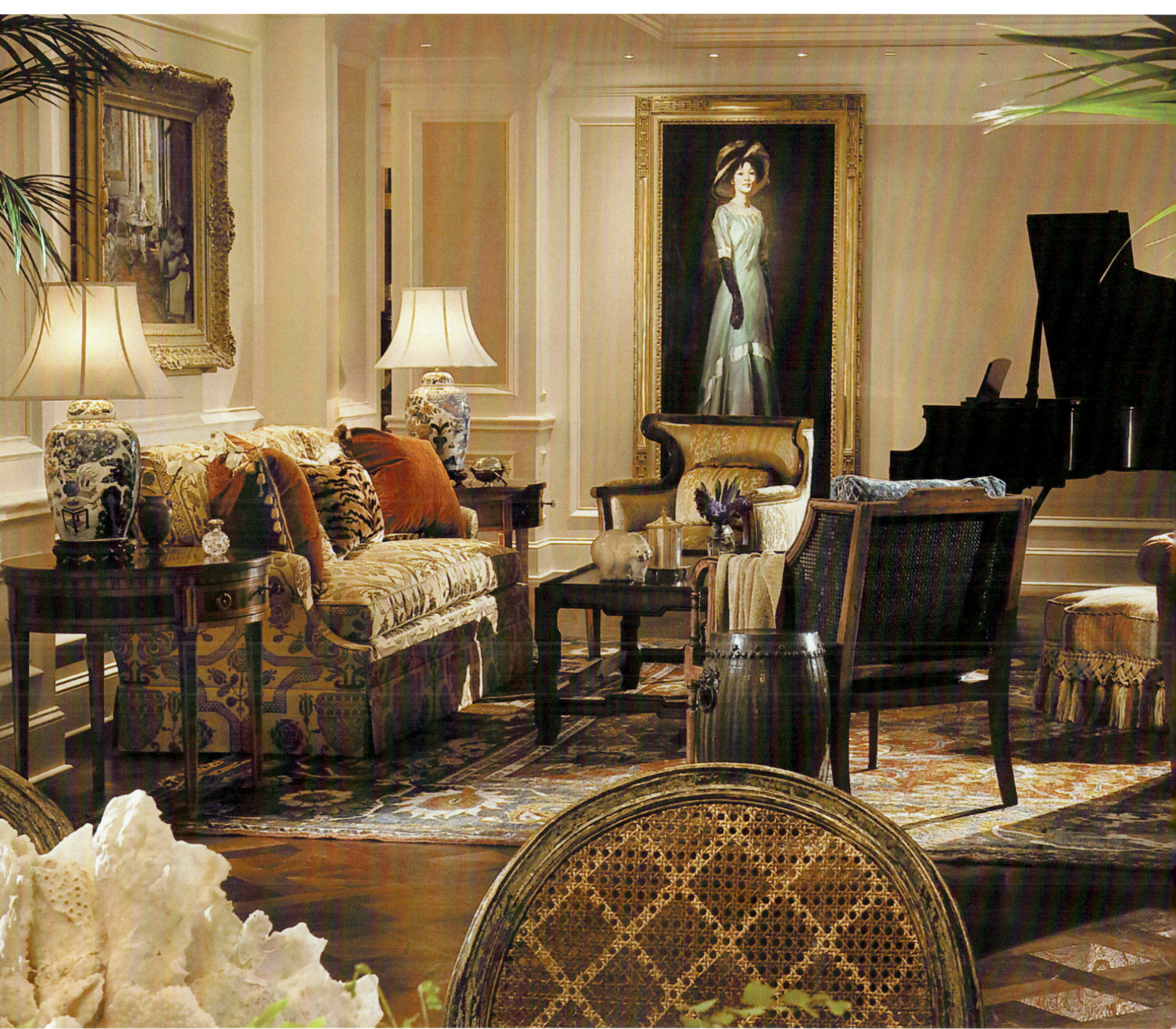

McGlothlin residence, Naples, Florida

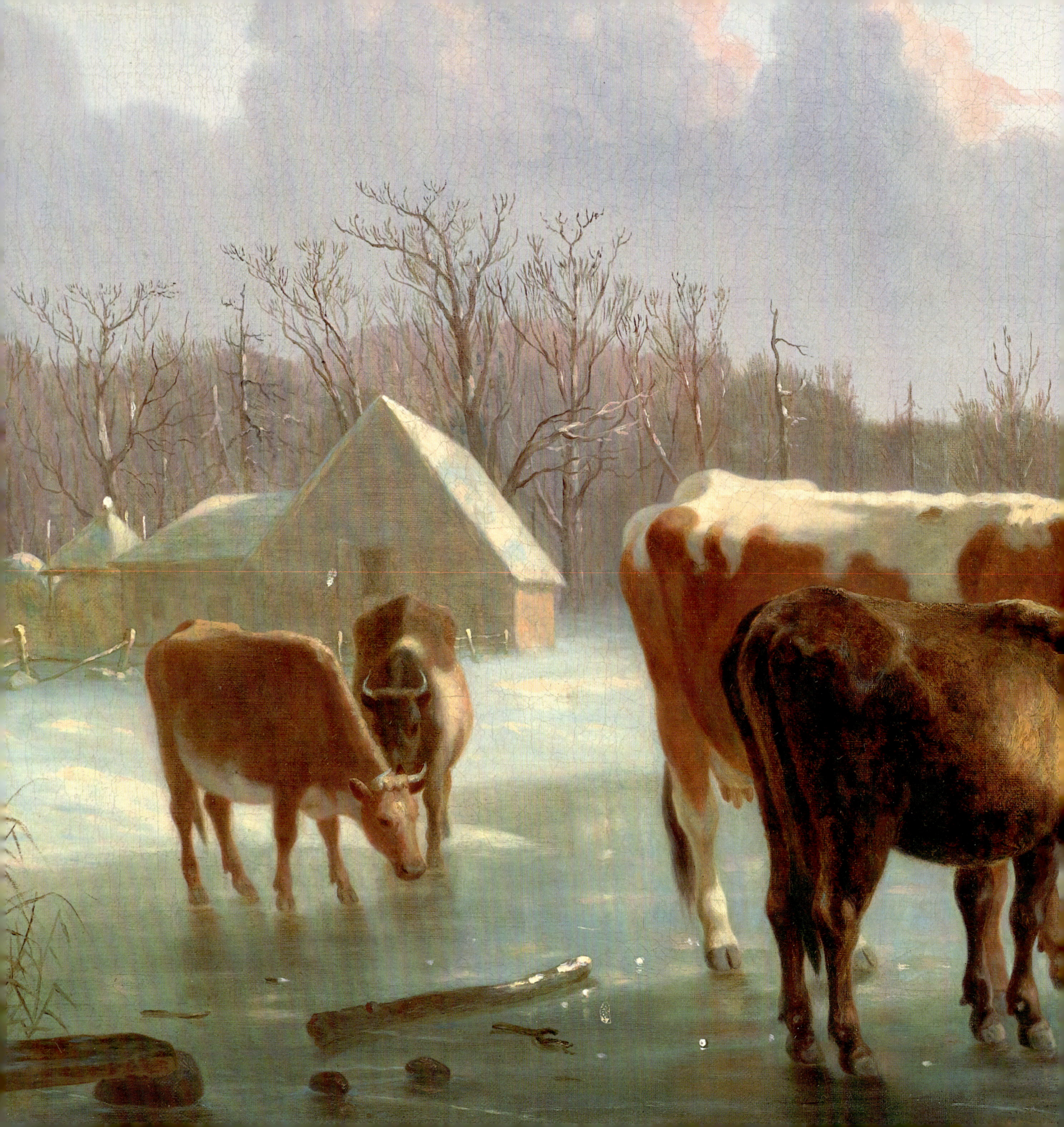

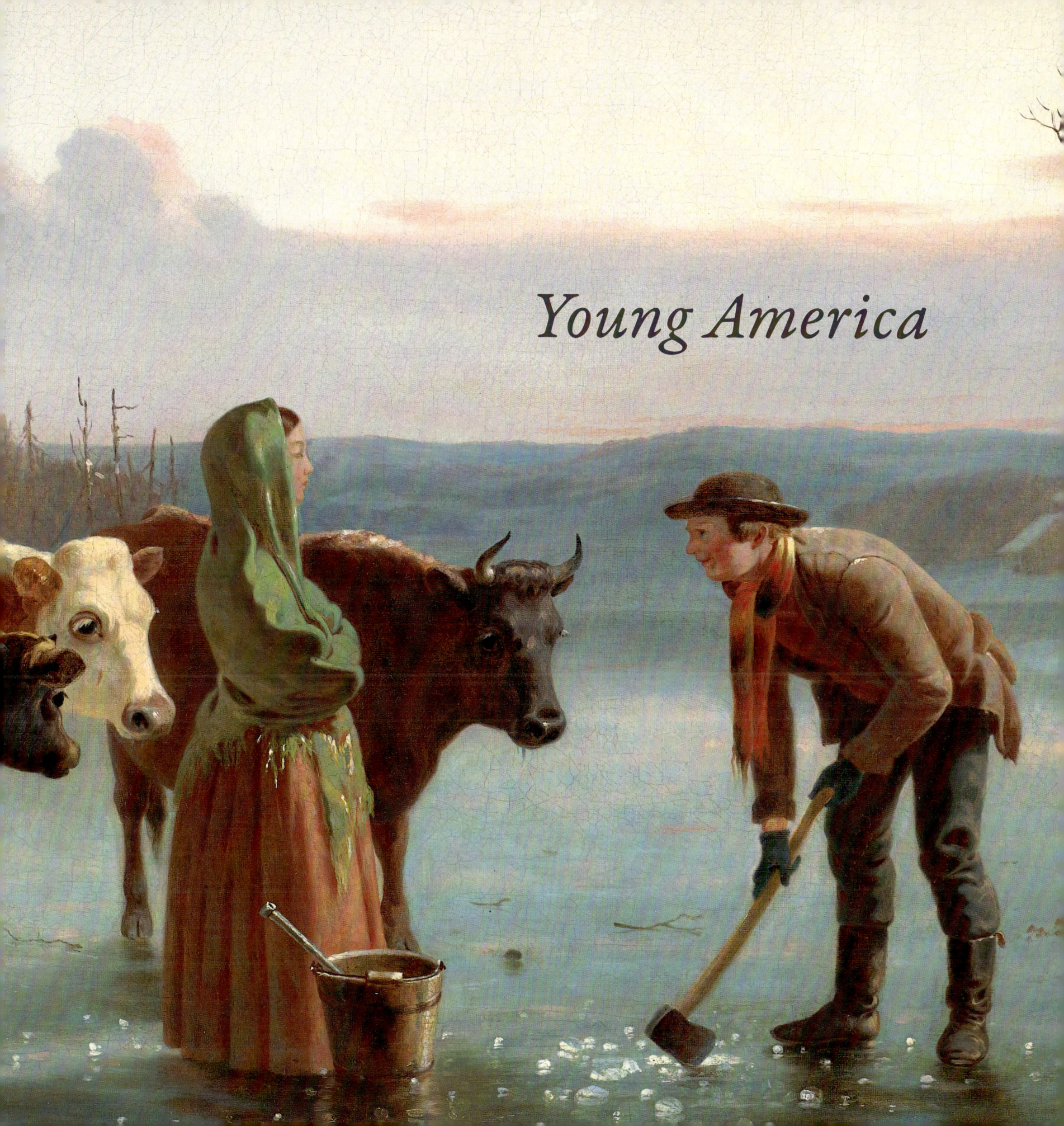

Young America

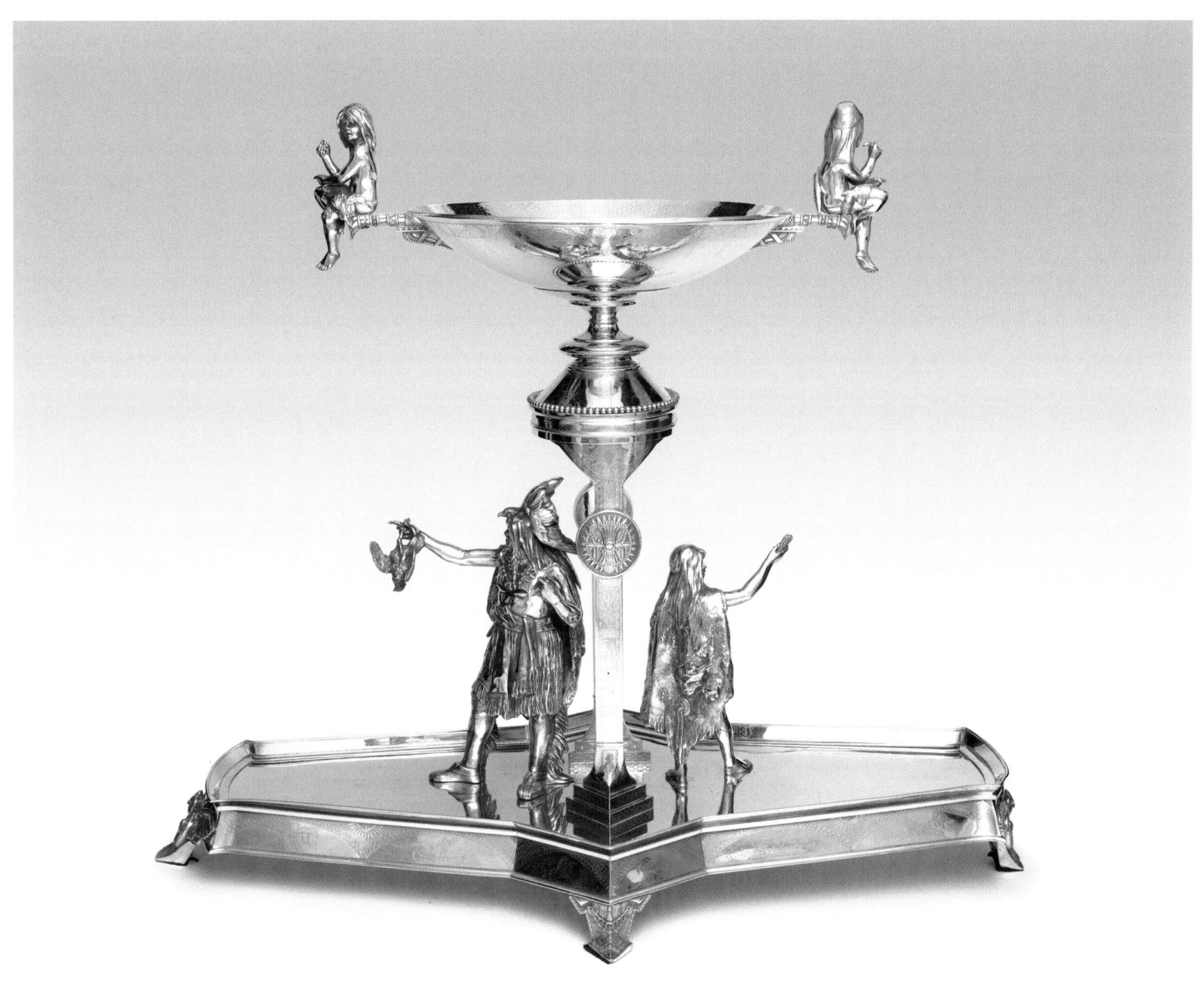

Attributed to Theodore Baur (1835–1898) for Meriden Britannia Company, **Chief and Squaw Centerpiece,** 1876
Silver-plated, 34 ½ x 41 x 19¼ inches

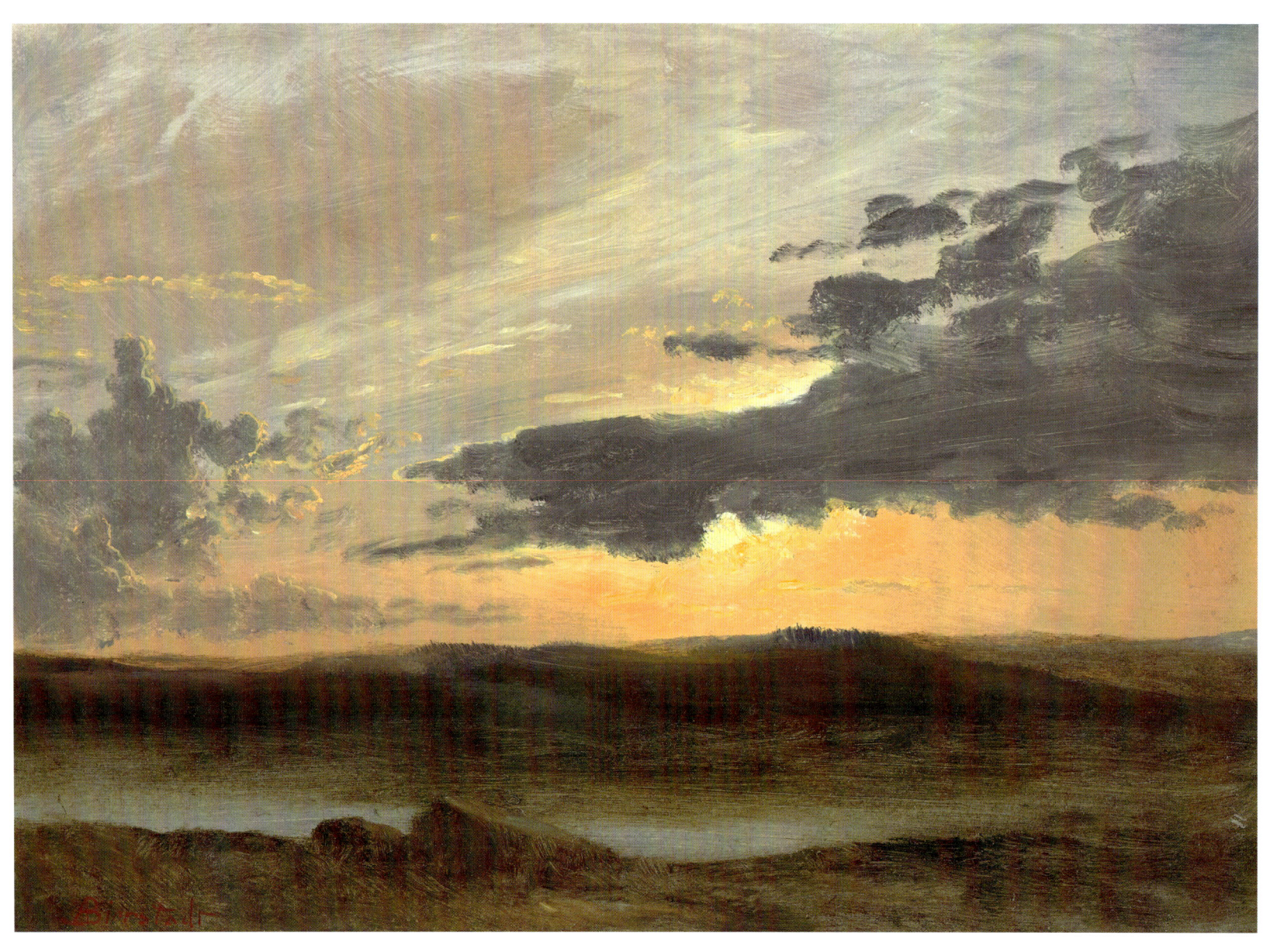

ALBERT BIERSTADT (1830–1902), **Evening,** ca. 1870, oil on paper, 11 x 15 ½ inches

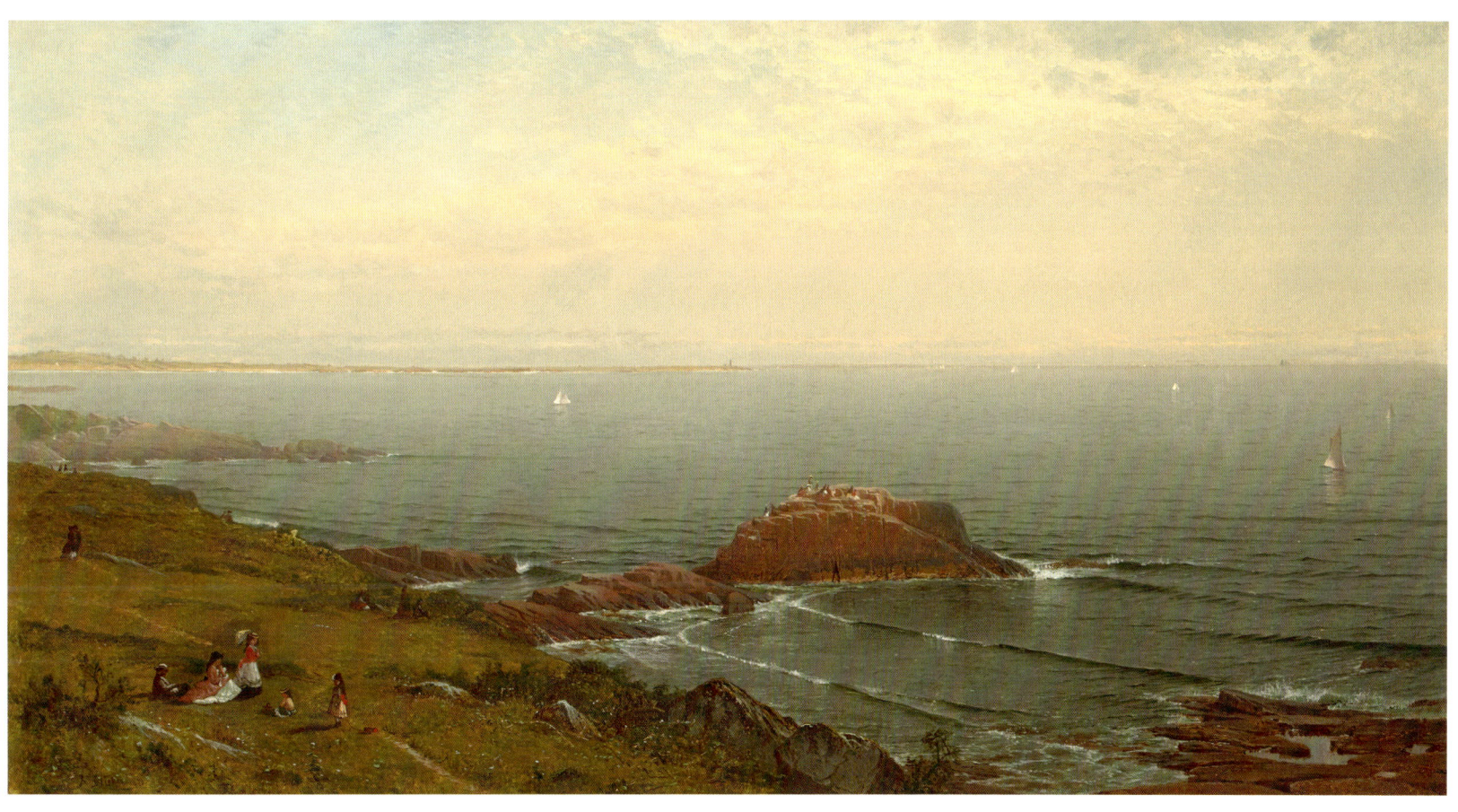

ALFRED THOMPSON BRICHER (1837–1908), **Indian Rock, Narragansett Bay,** 1871, oil on canvas, 27 x 50 inches

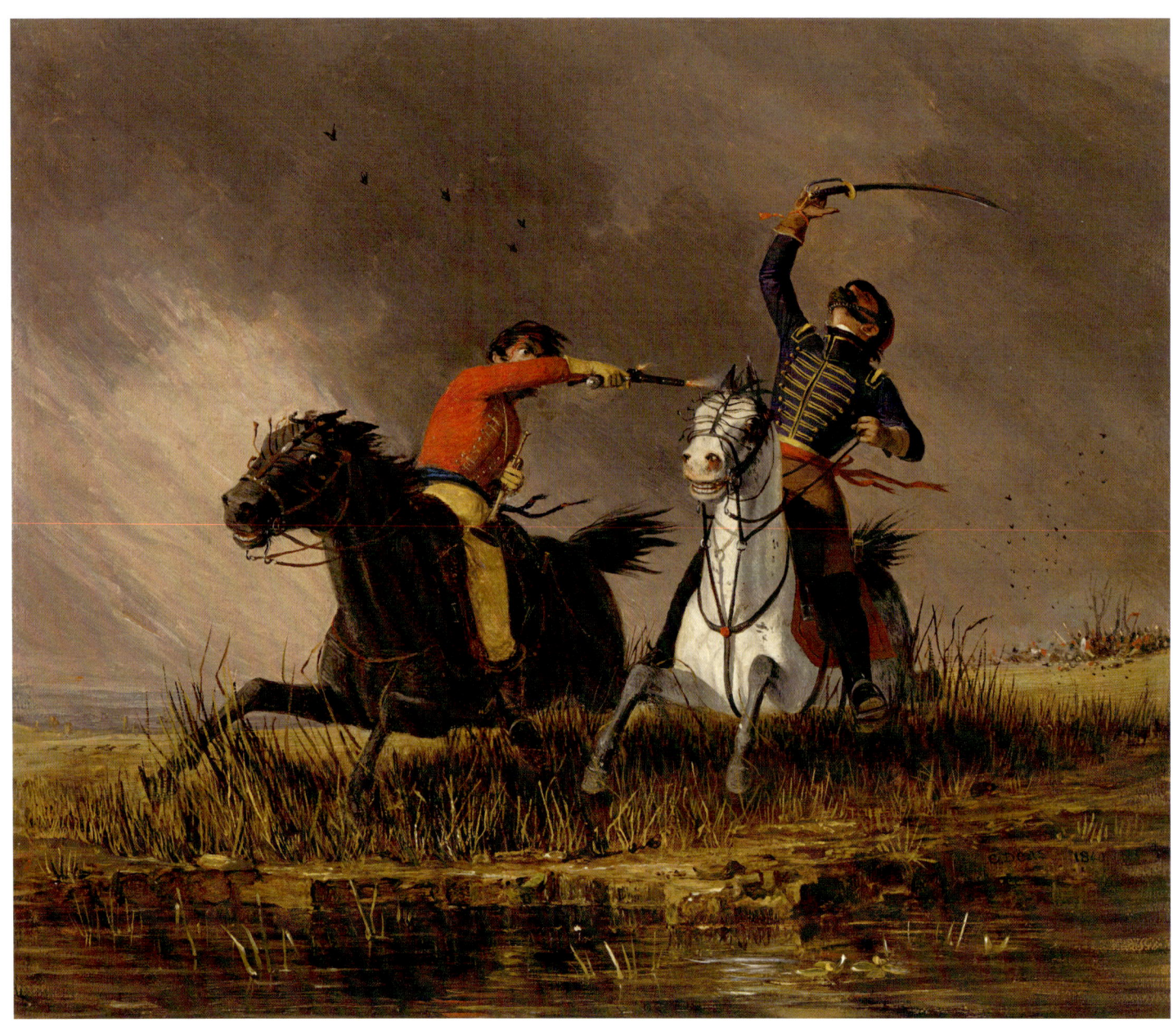

Charles Deas (1818–1867), **The Trooper,** 1840, oil on canvas, 12 ¼ x 14 inches

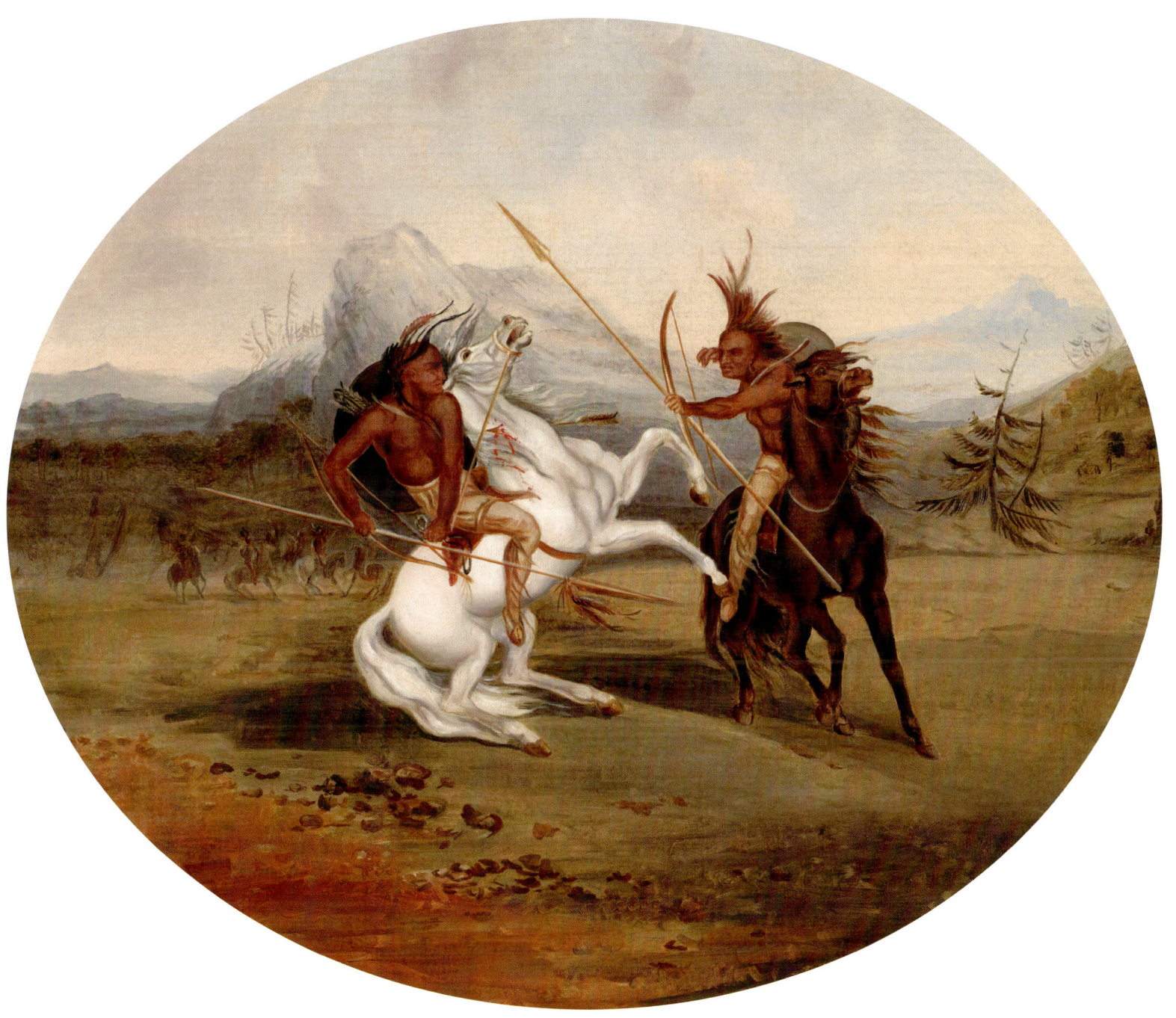

Attributed to JOHN H. DRURY (1816–after 1914), **Study for** *Dueling on the Missouri,* ca. 1852
Oil on canvas, 20 x 22 ½ inches

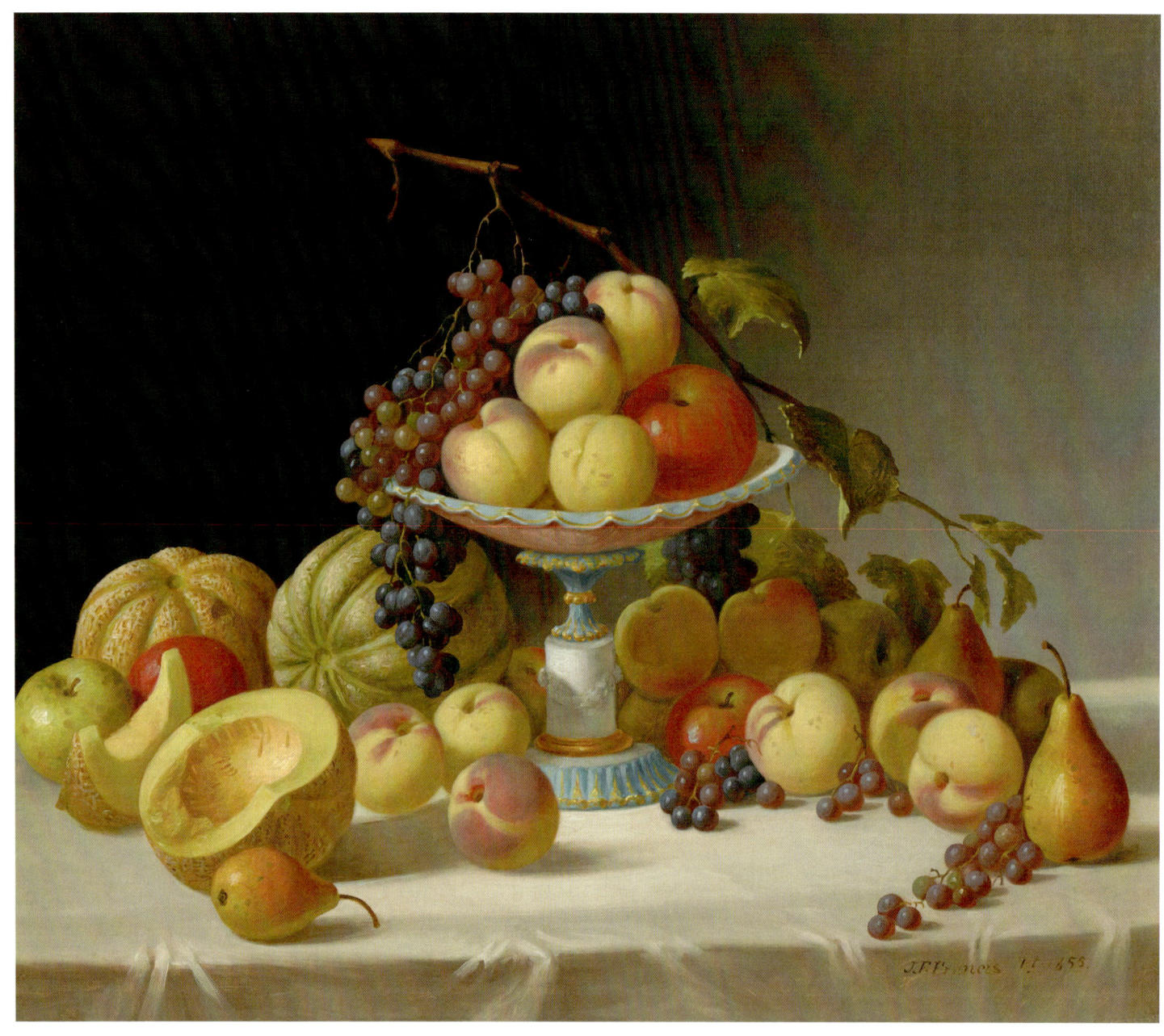

John F. Francis (1808–1886), **Still Life: Fruit and Wine Glass,** 1856, oil on canvas, 15 x 19 inches

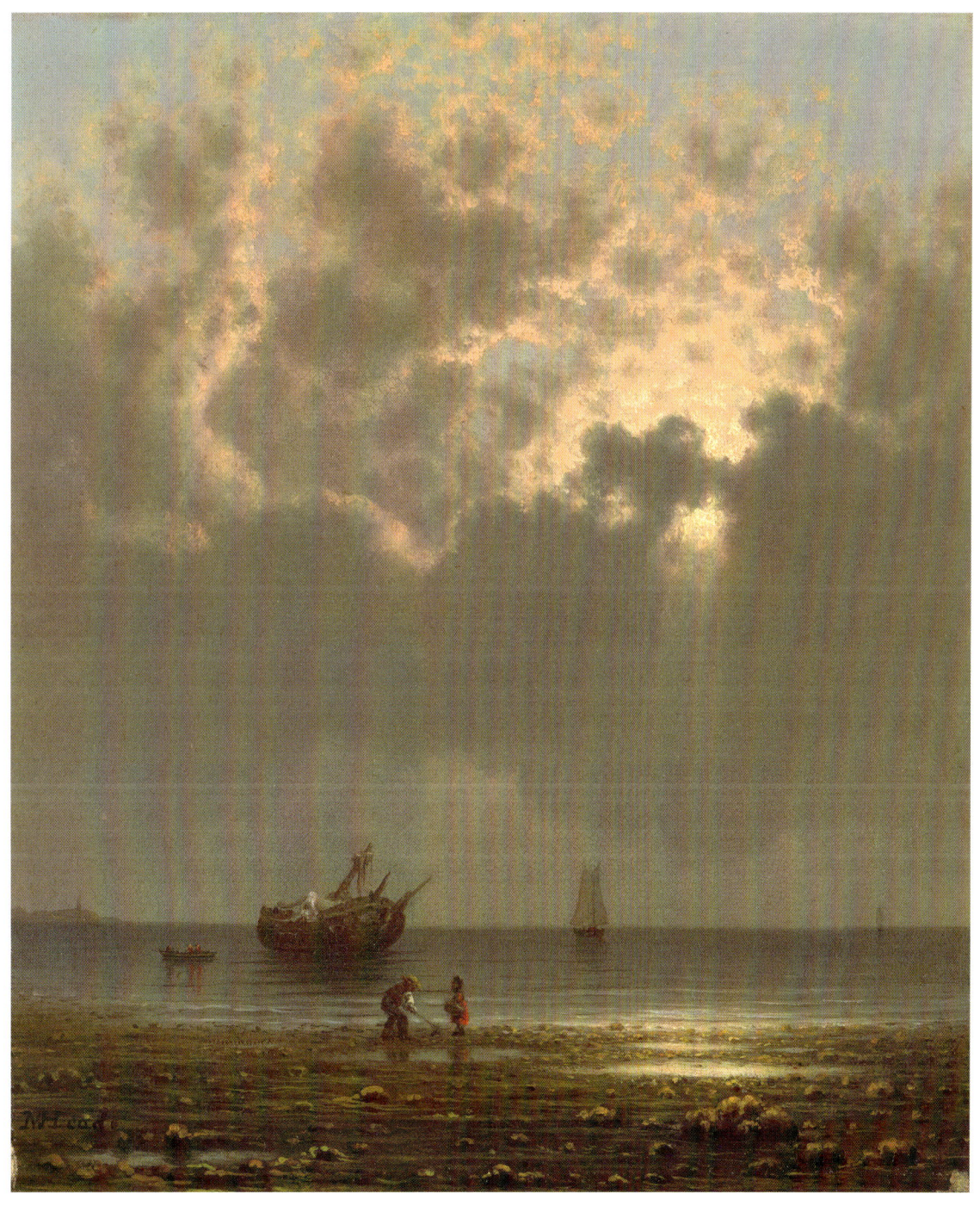

MARTIN JOHNSON HEADE (1819–1904), **Sun Breaking through the Clouds,** ca. 1866–70
Oil on canvas, 12½ x 10½ inches

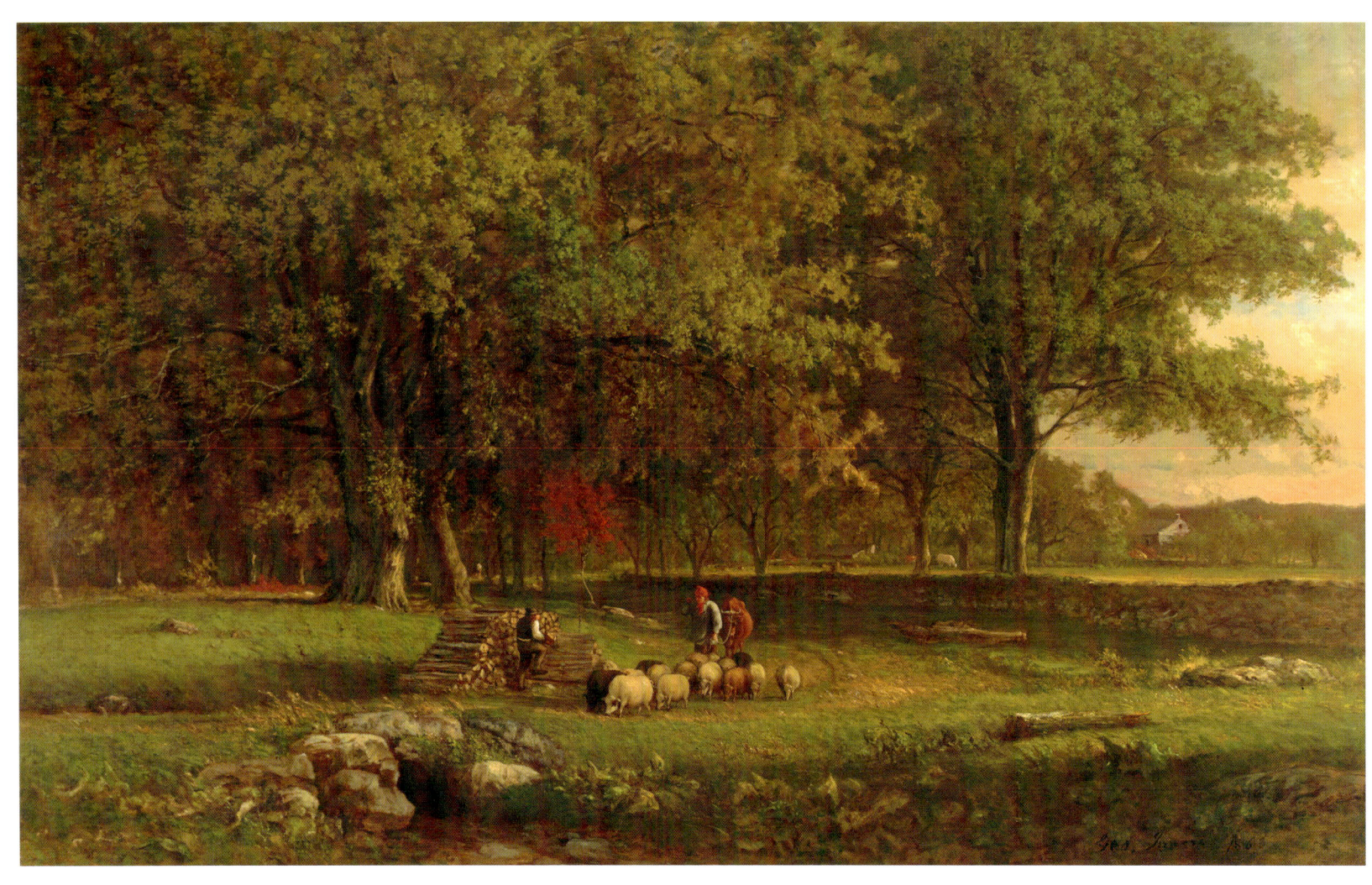

GEORGE INNESS (1825–1894), **Evening,** 1868, oil on canvas, 48 ½ x 78 ¼ inches

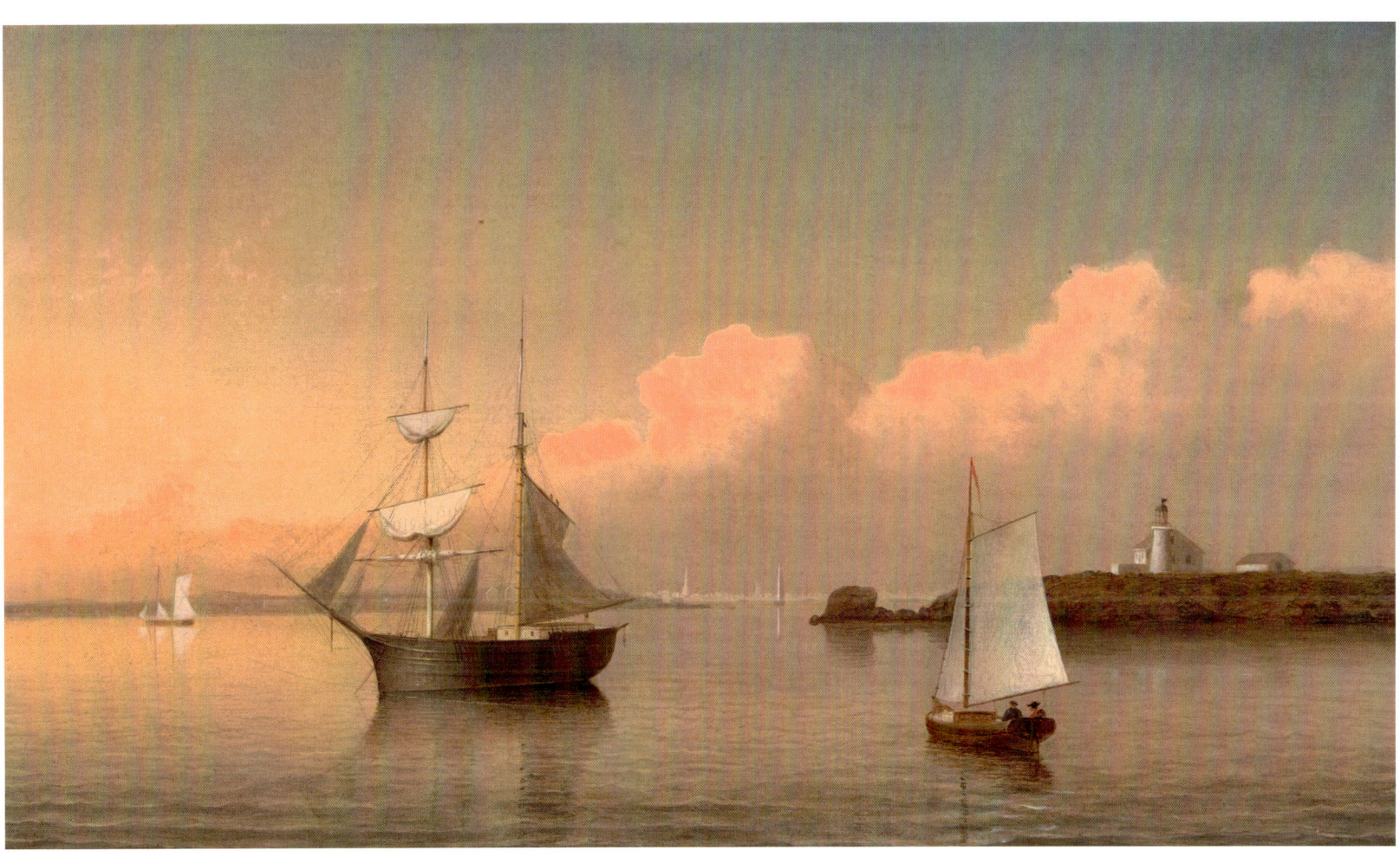

FITZ HENRY LANE (1804–1865), **Sunset off Ten Pound Island, Gloucester,** ca. 1860, oil on canvas, 12 x 20 inches

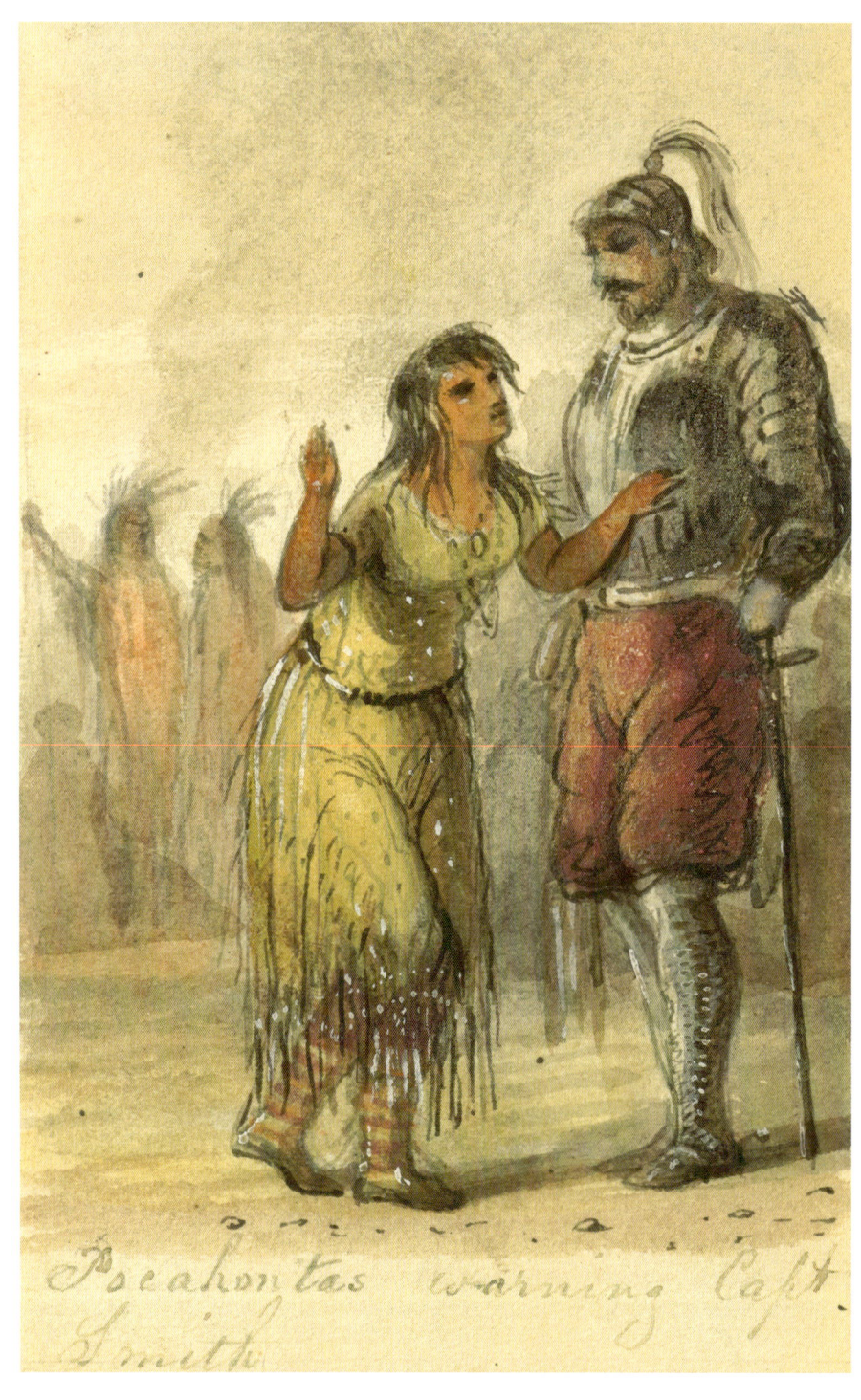

ALFRED JACOB MILLER (1810–1874), **Pocahontas Warning Captain John Smith,** 1840s
Watercolor, ink, and pencil on paper, 5 x 3 inches

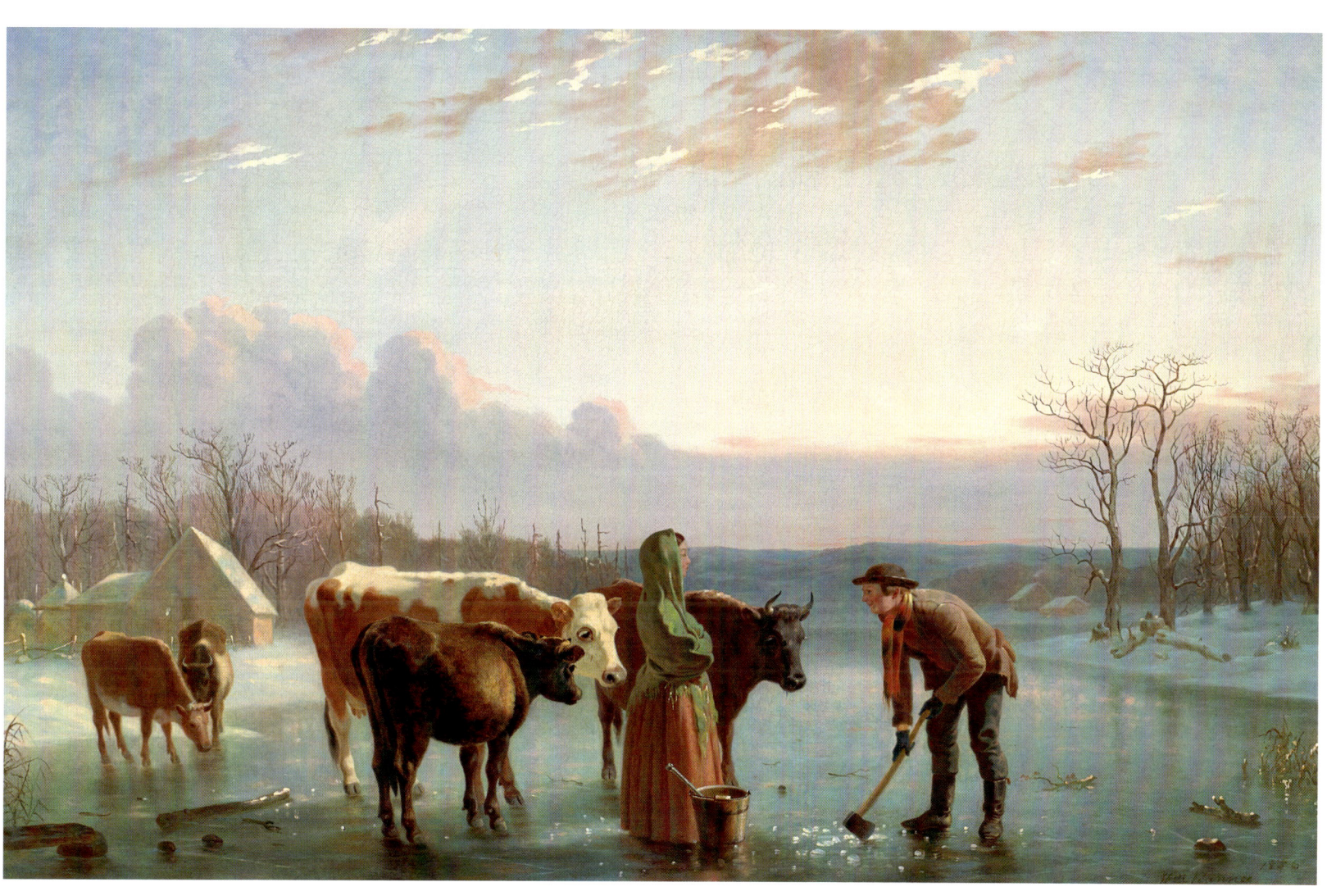

WILLIAM RANNEY (1813–1857), **Ice Gatherers,** 1850, oil on canvas, 22 x 35 inches

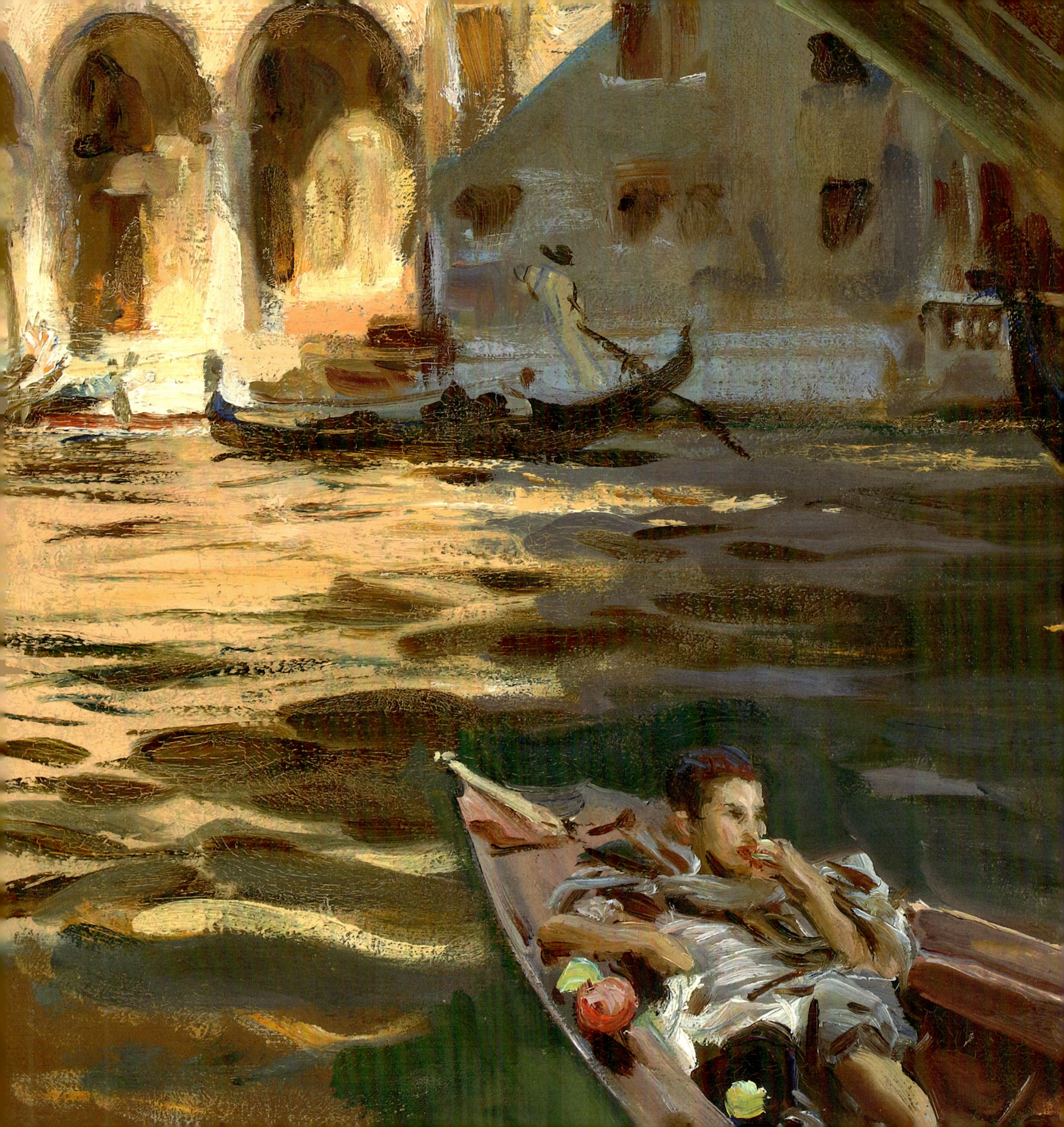

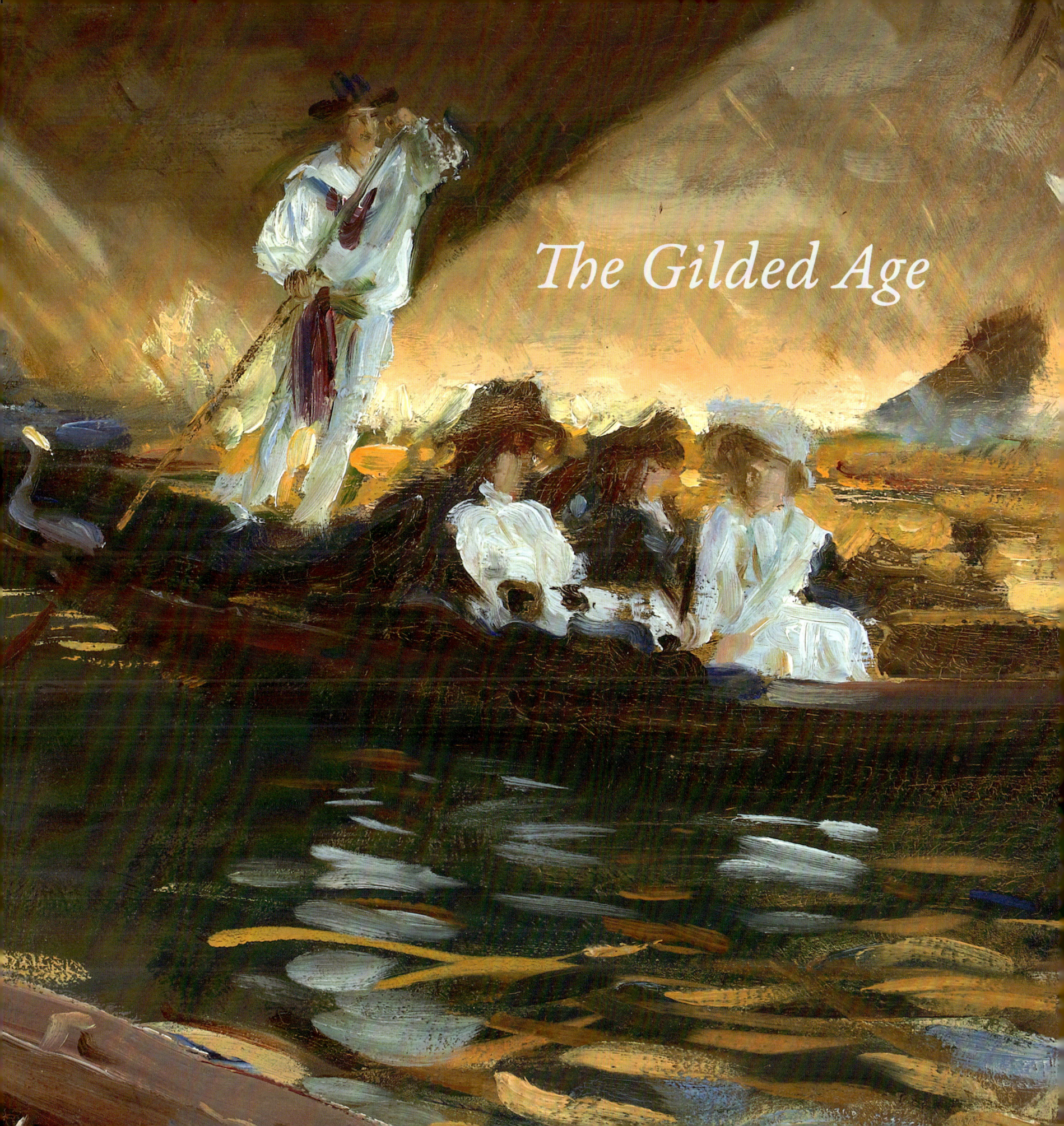

The Gilded Age

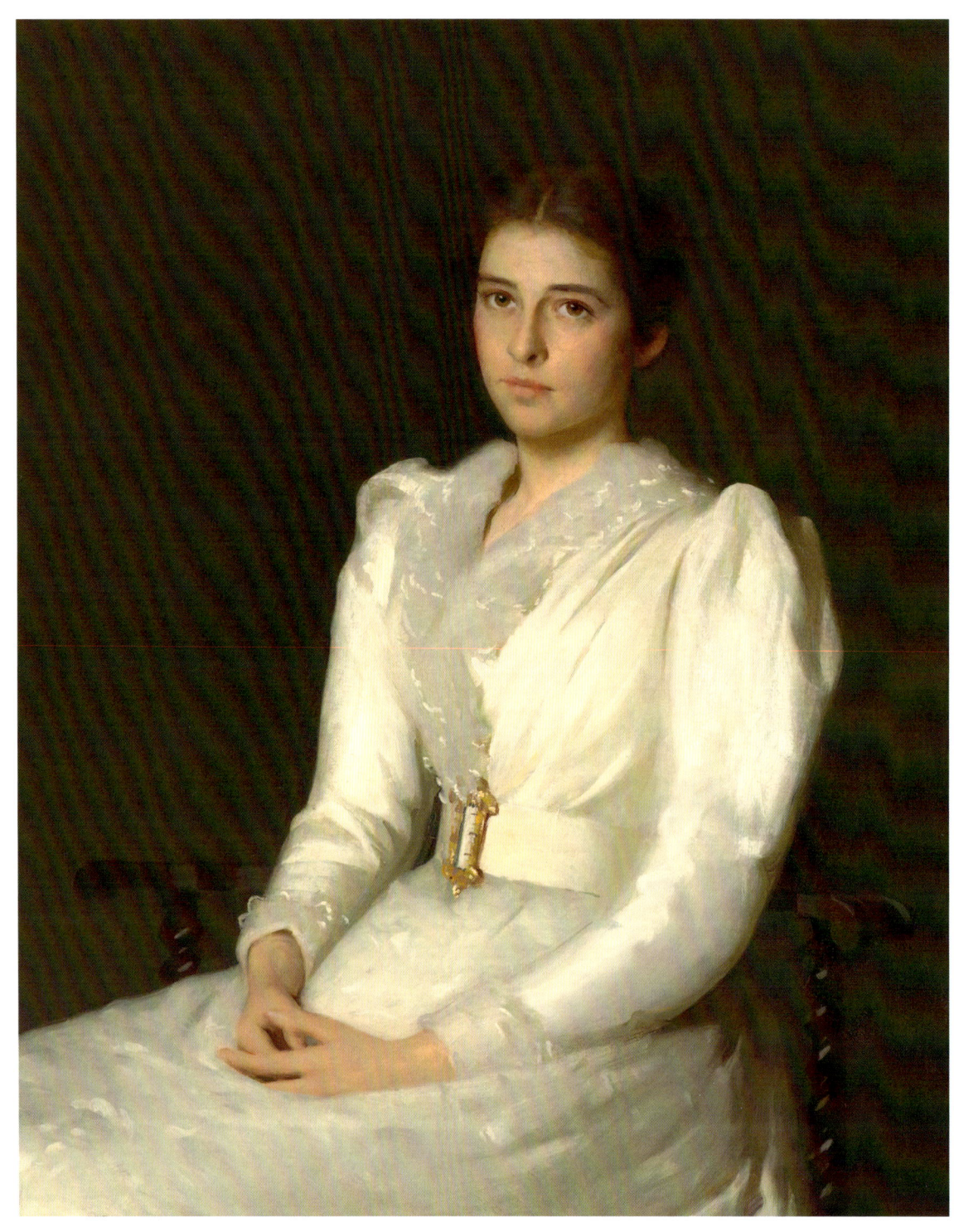

FRANK BENSON (1862–1951), **Alice Bacon (Mrs. Lothrop)**, 1891, oil on canvas, 36 x 29 inches

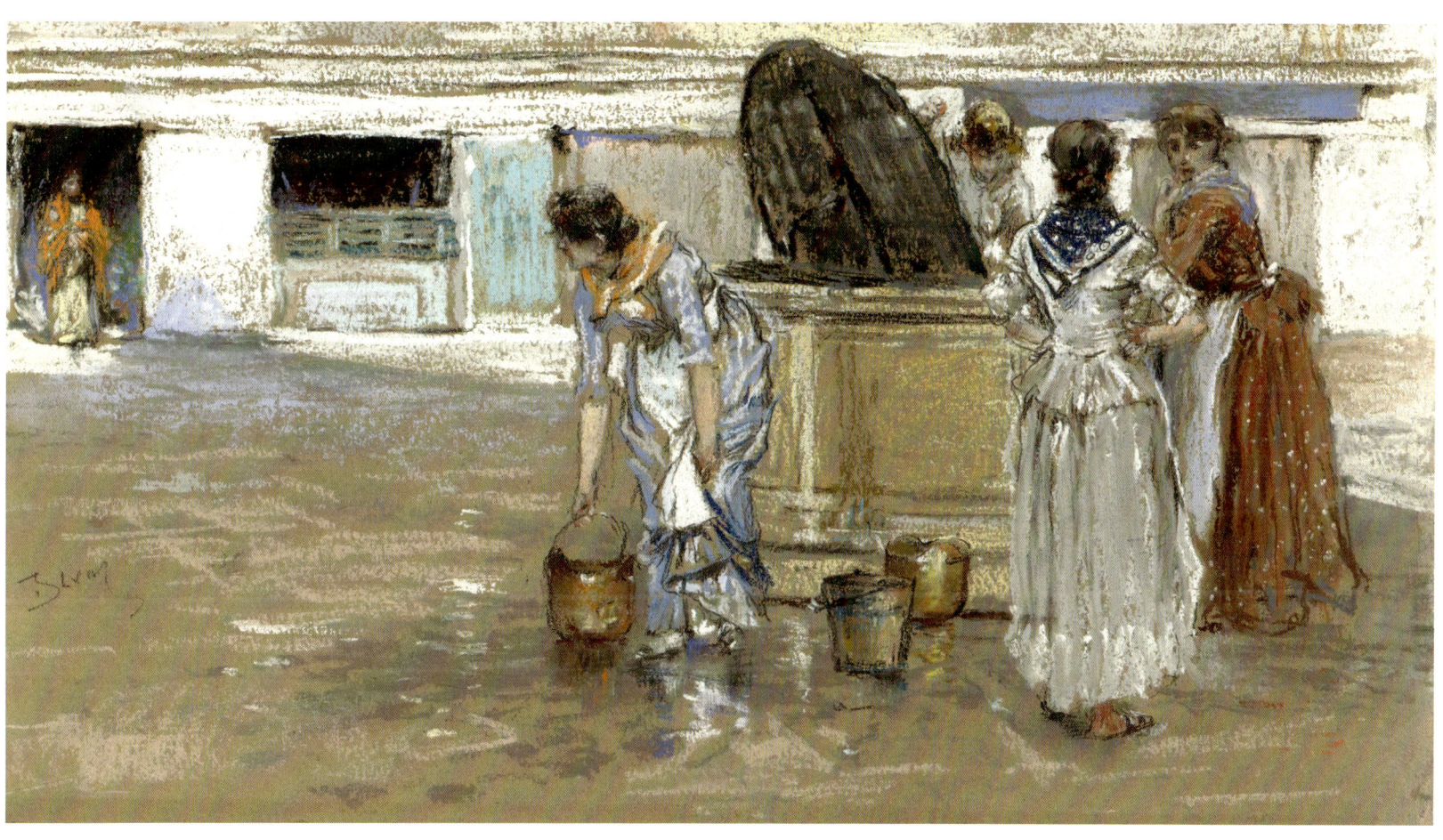

Robert Blum (1857–1903), **A Gossiping Place in Venice,** 1882, pastel on paper, 11 x 16 inches

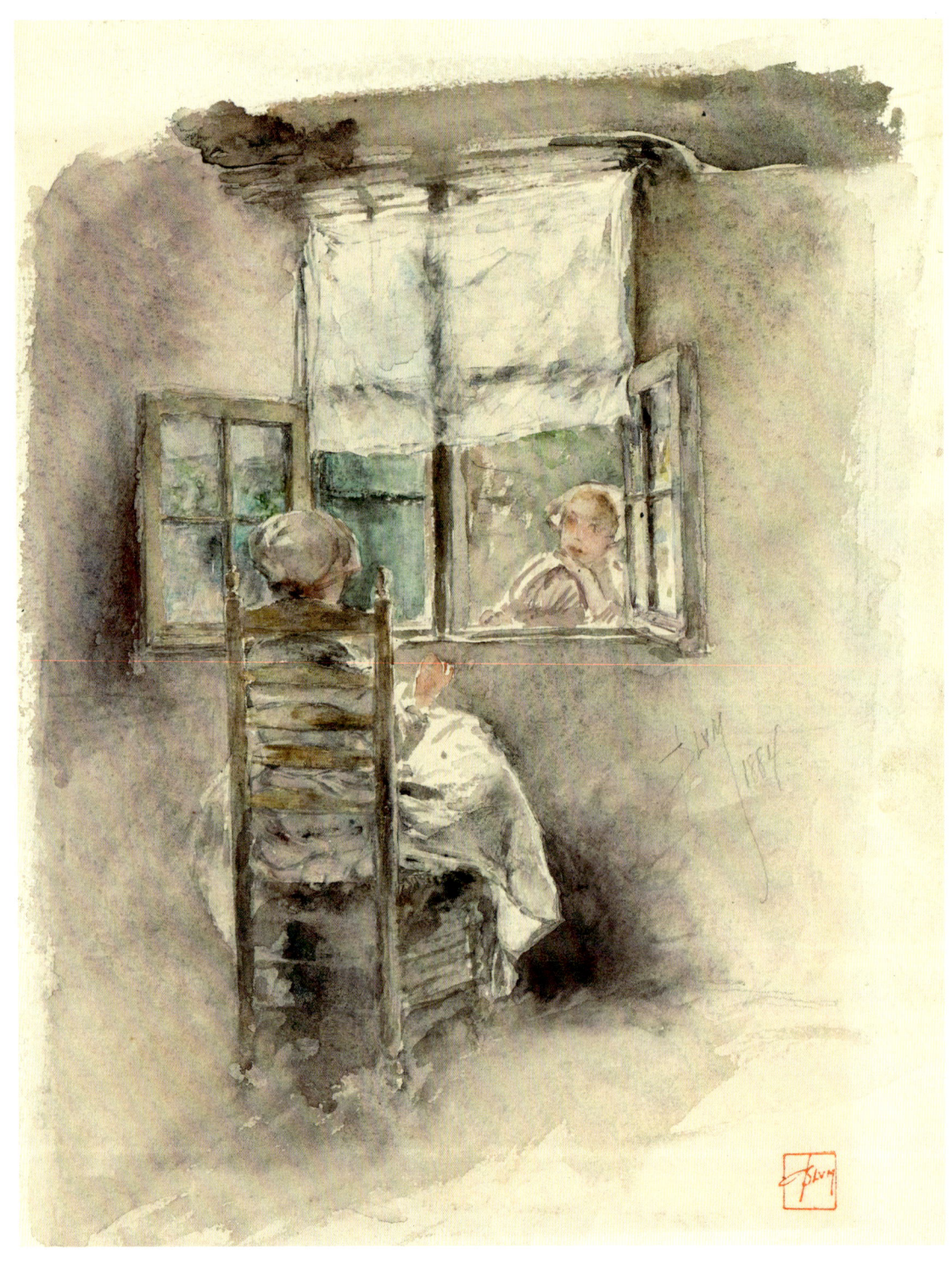

Robert Blum (1857–1903), **The Open Window,** 1884, watercolor on paper, 10 ¾ x 8 inches

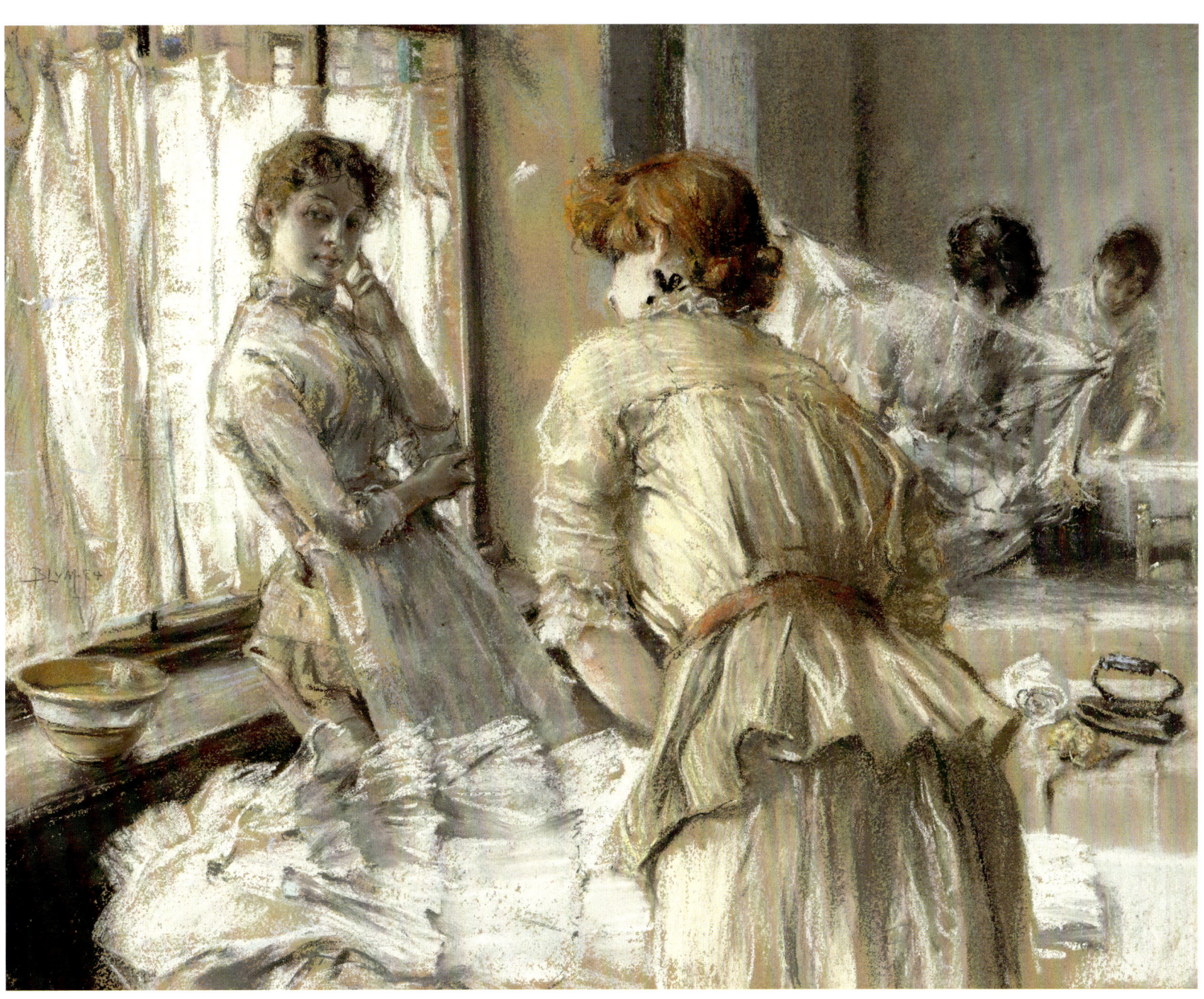

Robert Blum (1857–1903), **In the Laundry,** 1884, pastel on paper, 15 x 19 inches

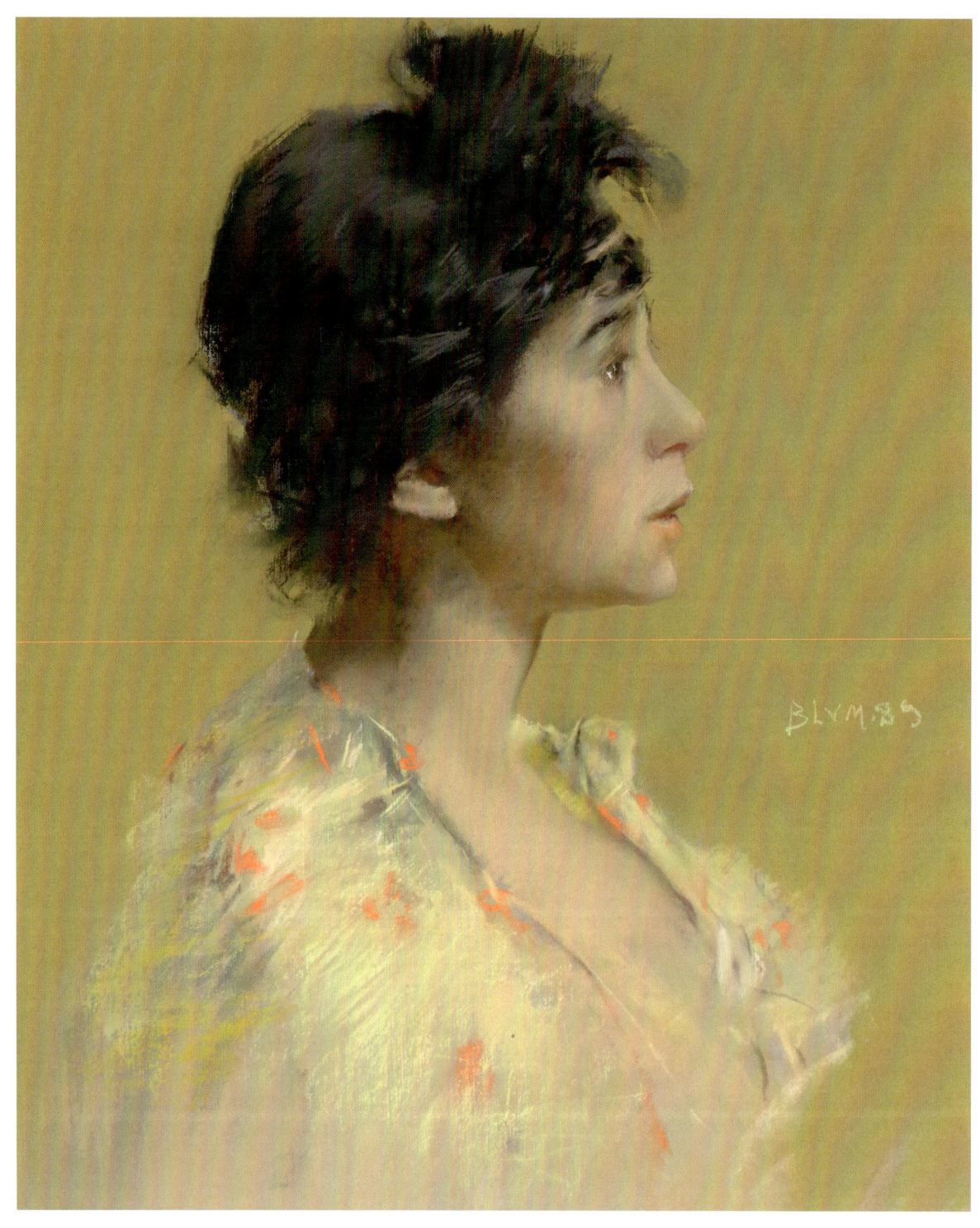

Robert Blum (1857–1903), **Flora de Stephano, the Artist's Model,** 1889, pastel on paper, 20 ½ x 18 ¼ inches

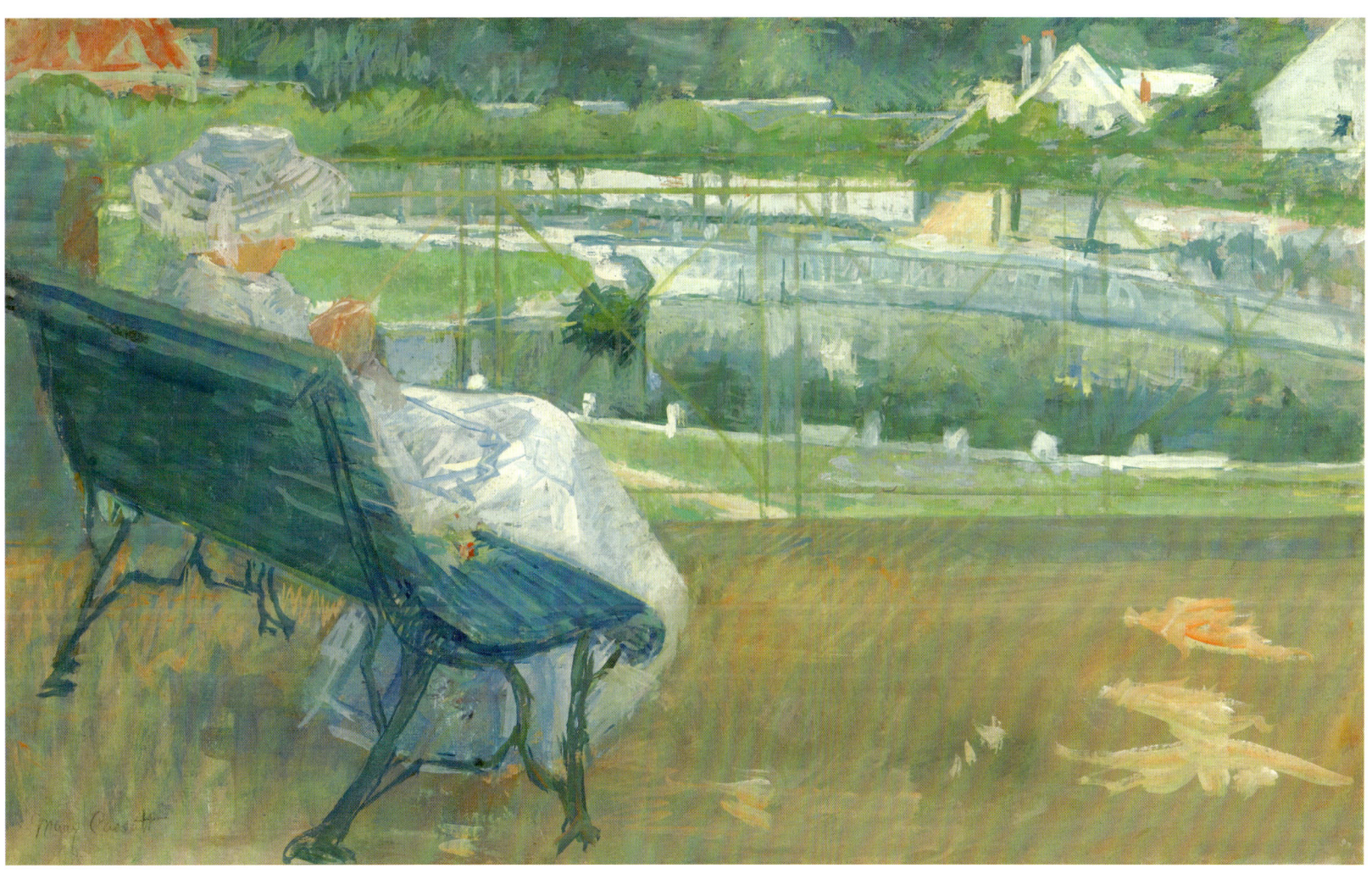

MARY CASSATT (1844–1926), **Lydia Seated on a Porch, Crocheting,** ca. 1882, oil with tempera on canvas, 15 x 24 ¼ inches

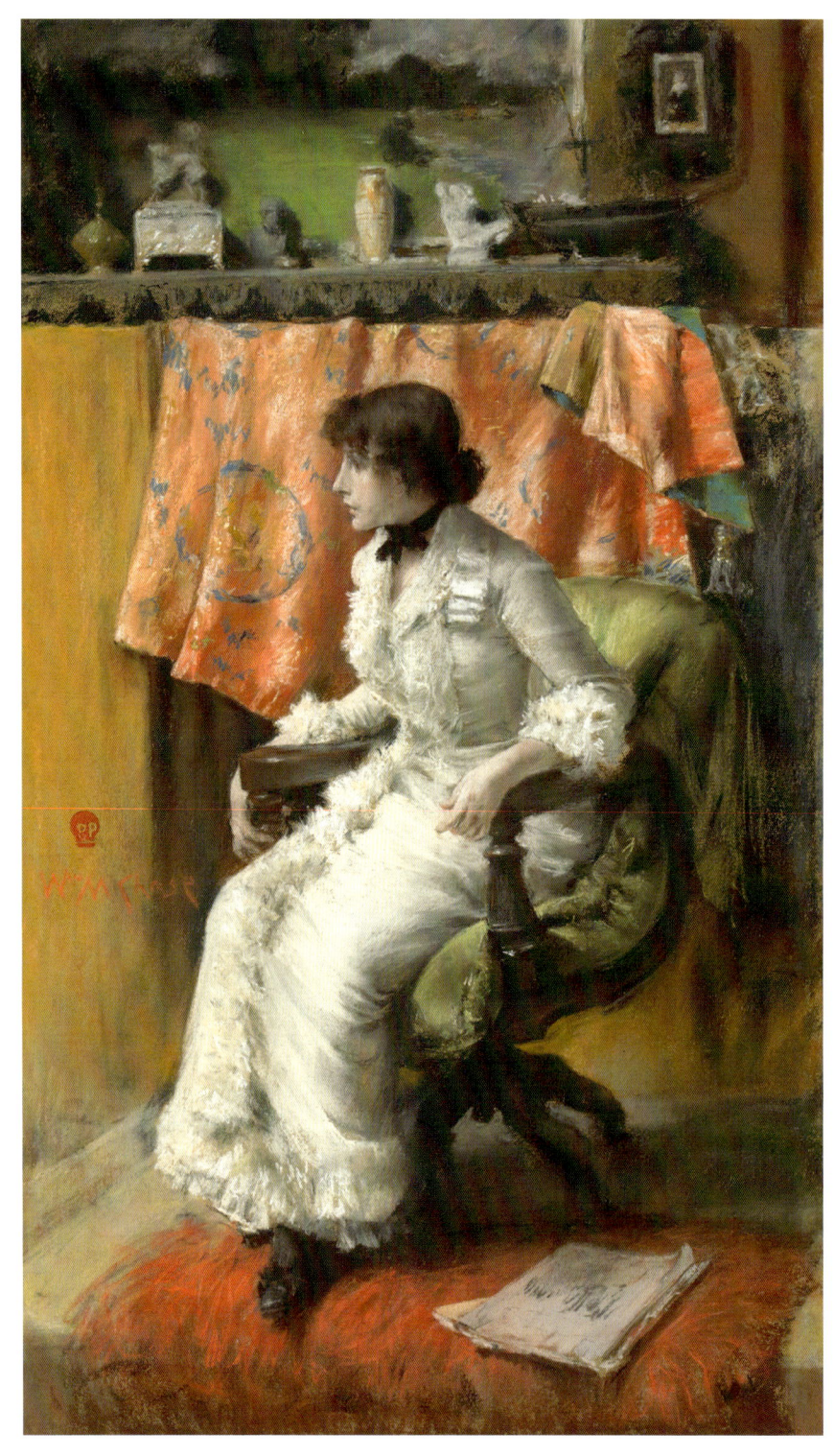

WILLIAM MERRITT CHASE (1849–1916), **In the Studio,** 1884
Pastel on paper, 39 x 22 ½ inches

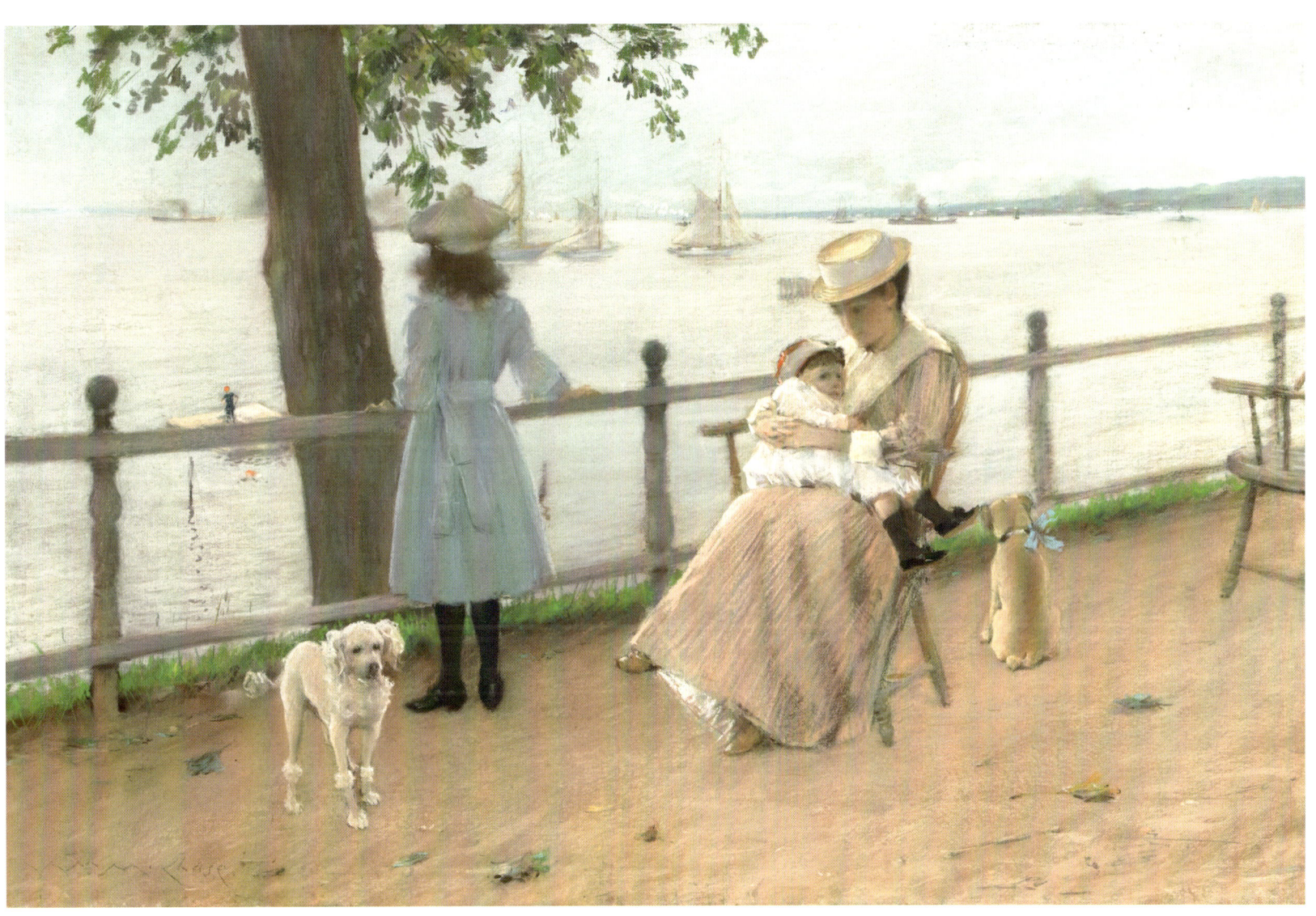

WILLIAM MERRITT CHASE (1849–1916), **Gravesend Bay, Afternoon by the Sea,** 1888, pastel on linen, 20 ¼ x 29 ½ inches

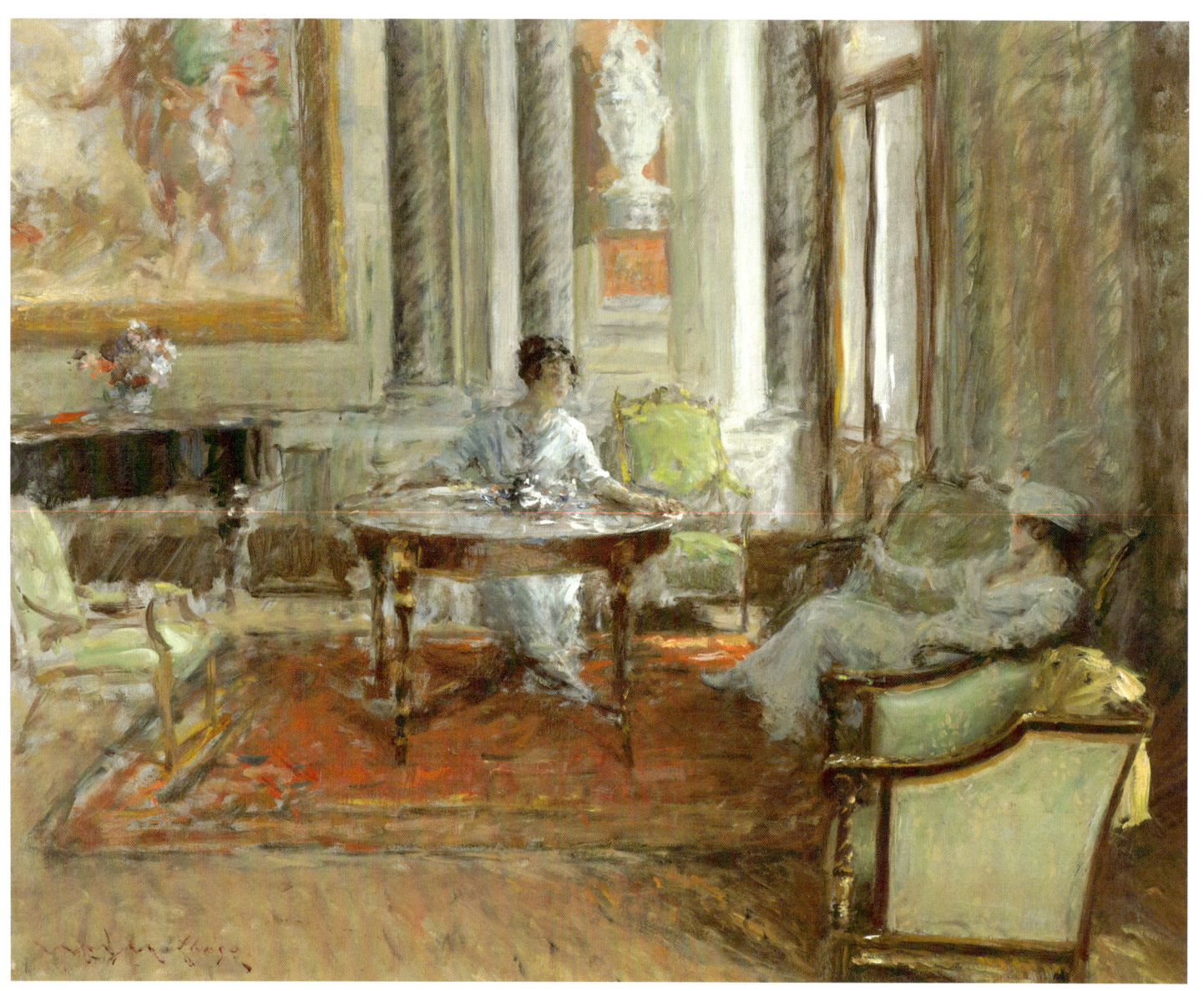

WILLIAM MERRITT CHASE (1849–1916), **Friendly Advice,** 1913, oil on canvas, 30 x 36 inches

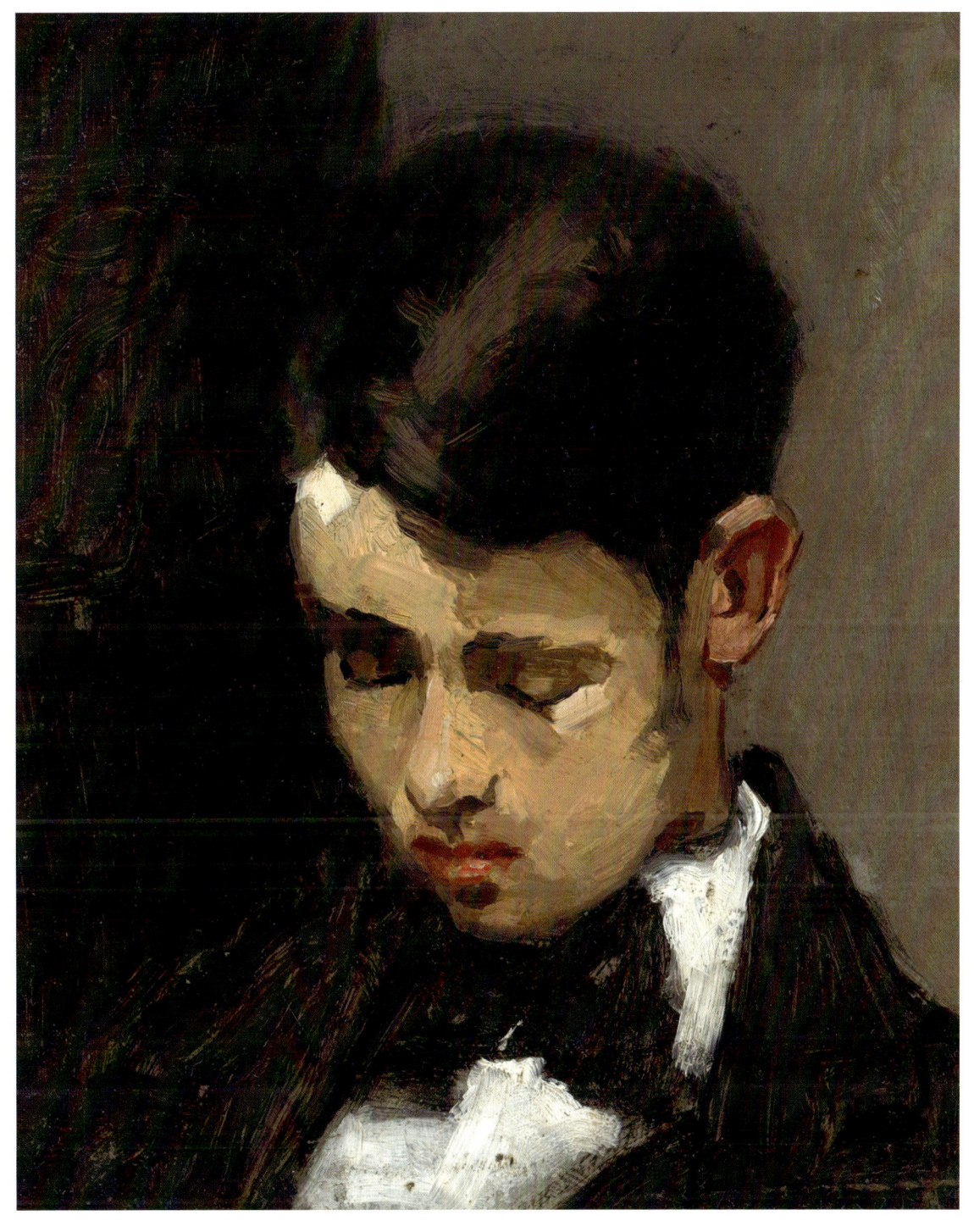

THOMAS EAKINS (1844–1916), **Portrait of Harry W. Barnitz,** 1884
Oil on board, 9 ³/₁₀ x 7 ¹/₅ inches

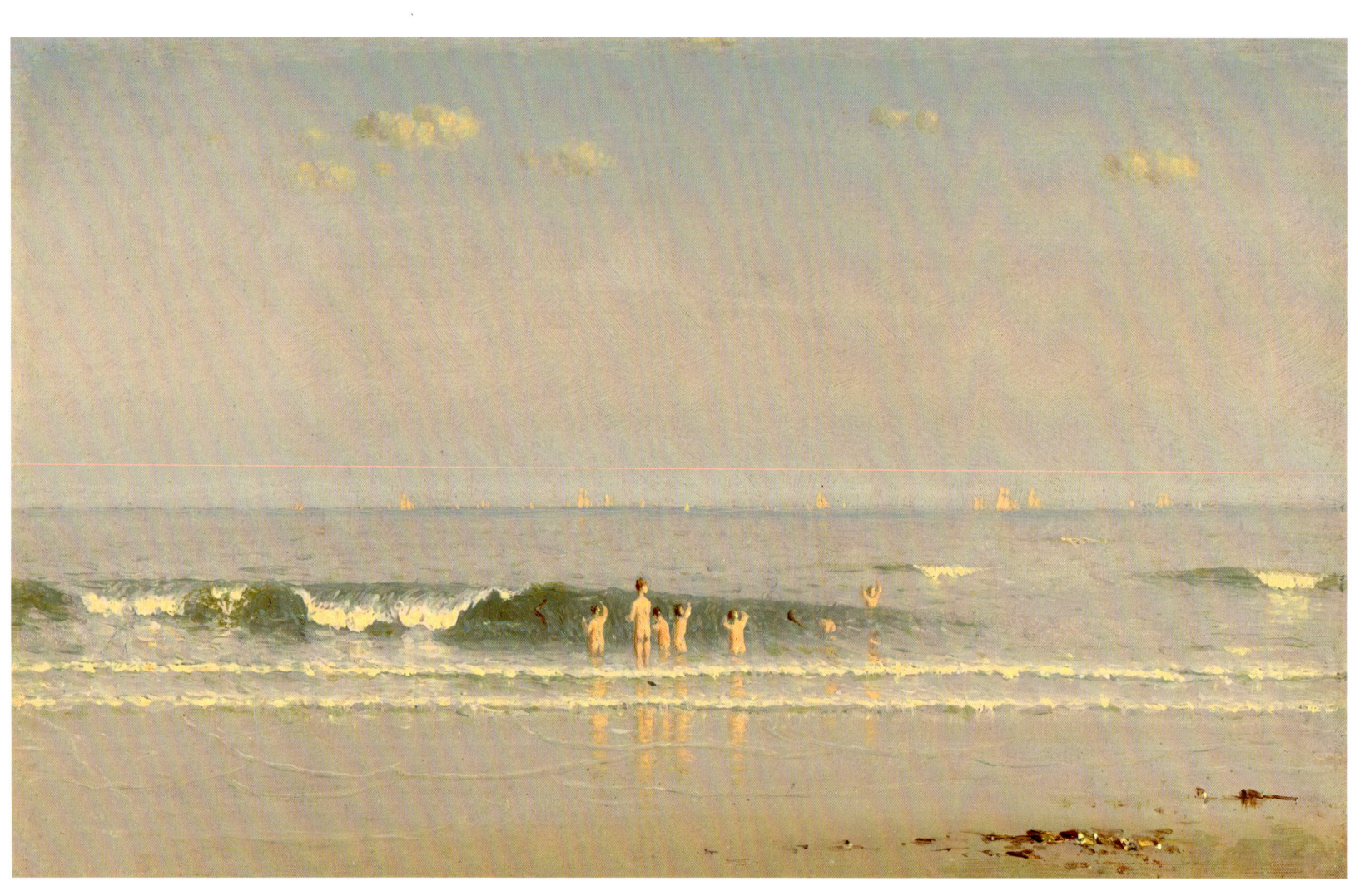

SANFORD GIFFORD (1823–1880), **On the Seashore Looking Eastward,** ca. 1878, oil on canvas, 9 x 16 inches

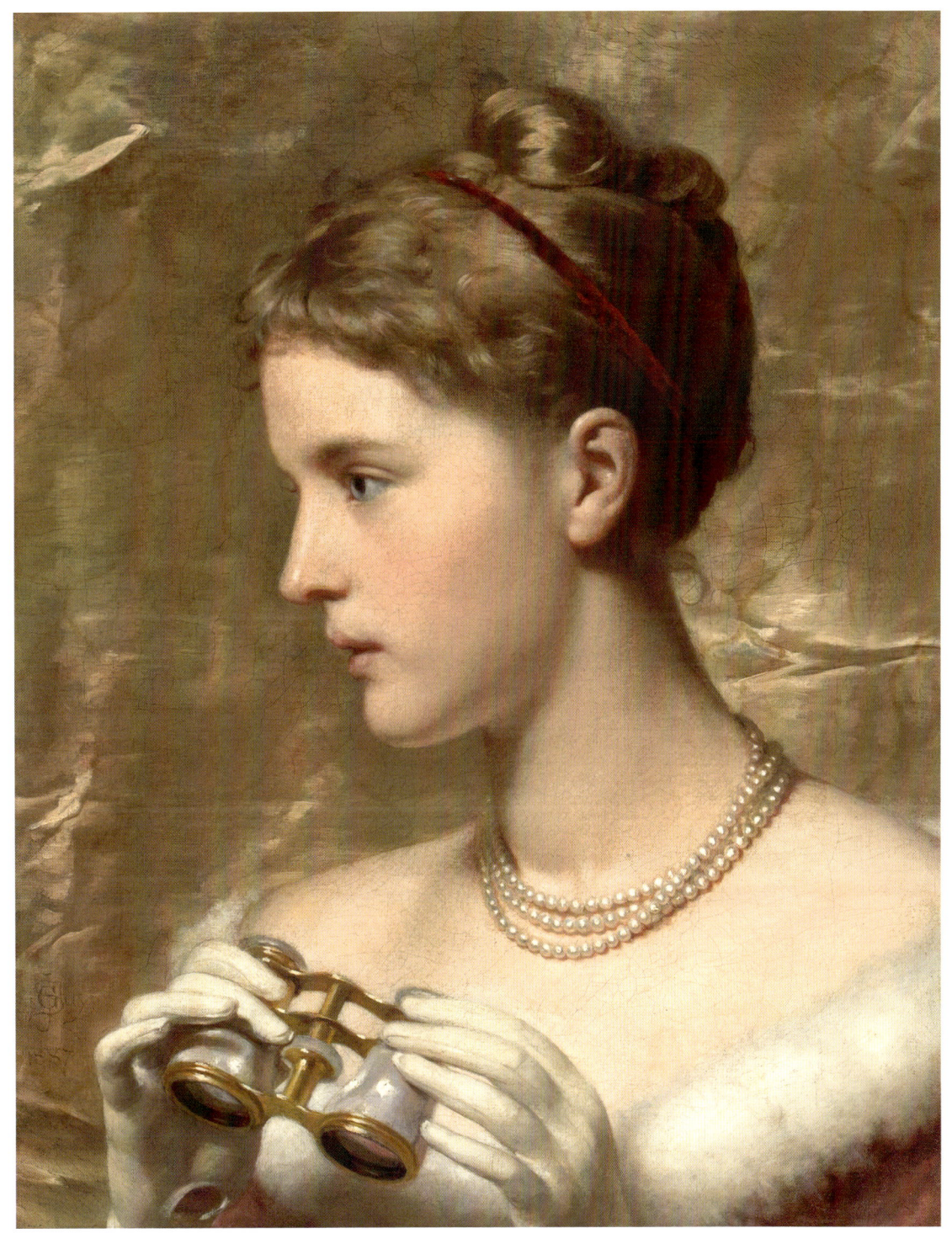

SEYMOUR GUY (1824–1910), **At the Opera,** 1887, oil on canvas, 19¼ x 15 inches

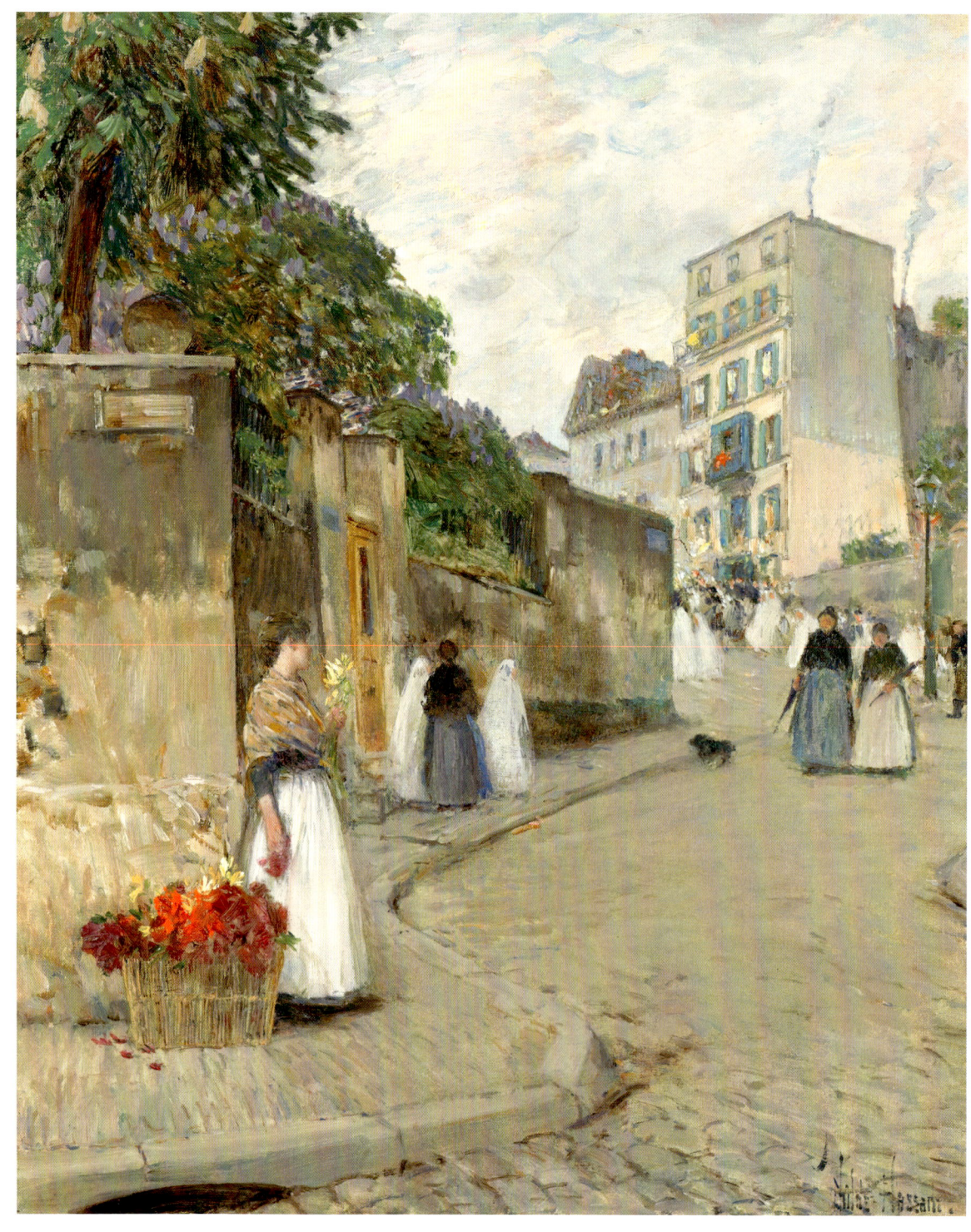

CHILDE HASSAM (1859–1935), **Rue Montmarte, Paris,** 1888, oil on canvas, 18 x 15 inches

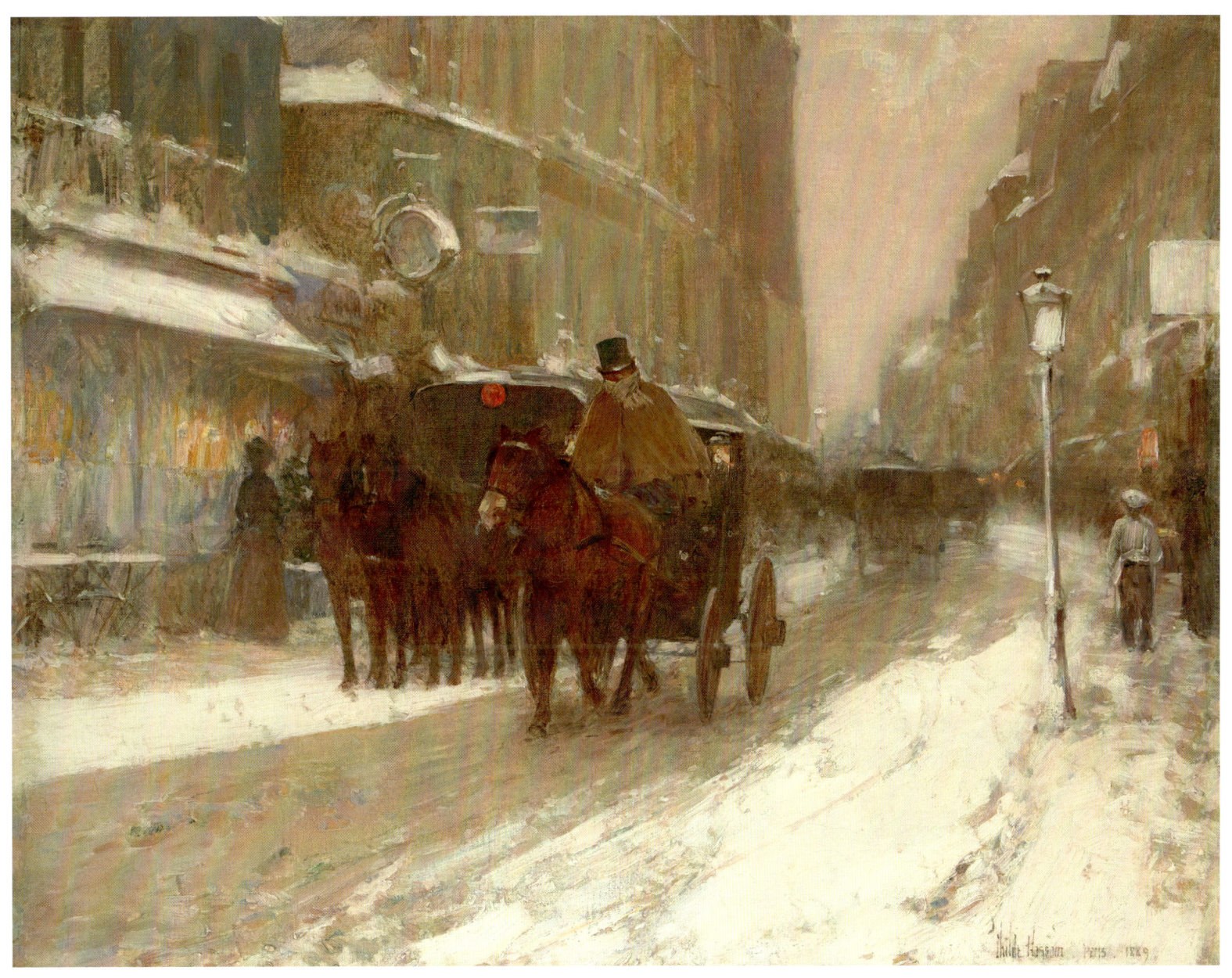

CHILDE HASSAM (1859–1935), **Winter Nightfall in the City,** 1889, oil on canvas, 25 ½ x 33 inches

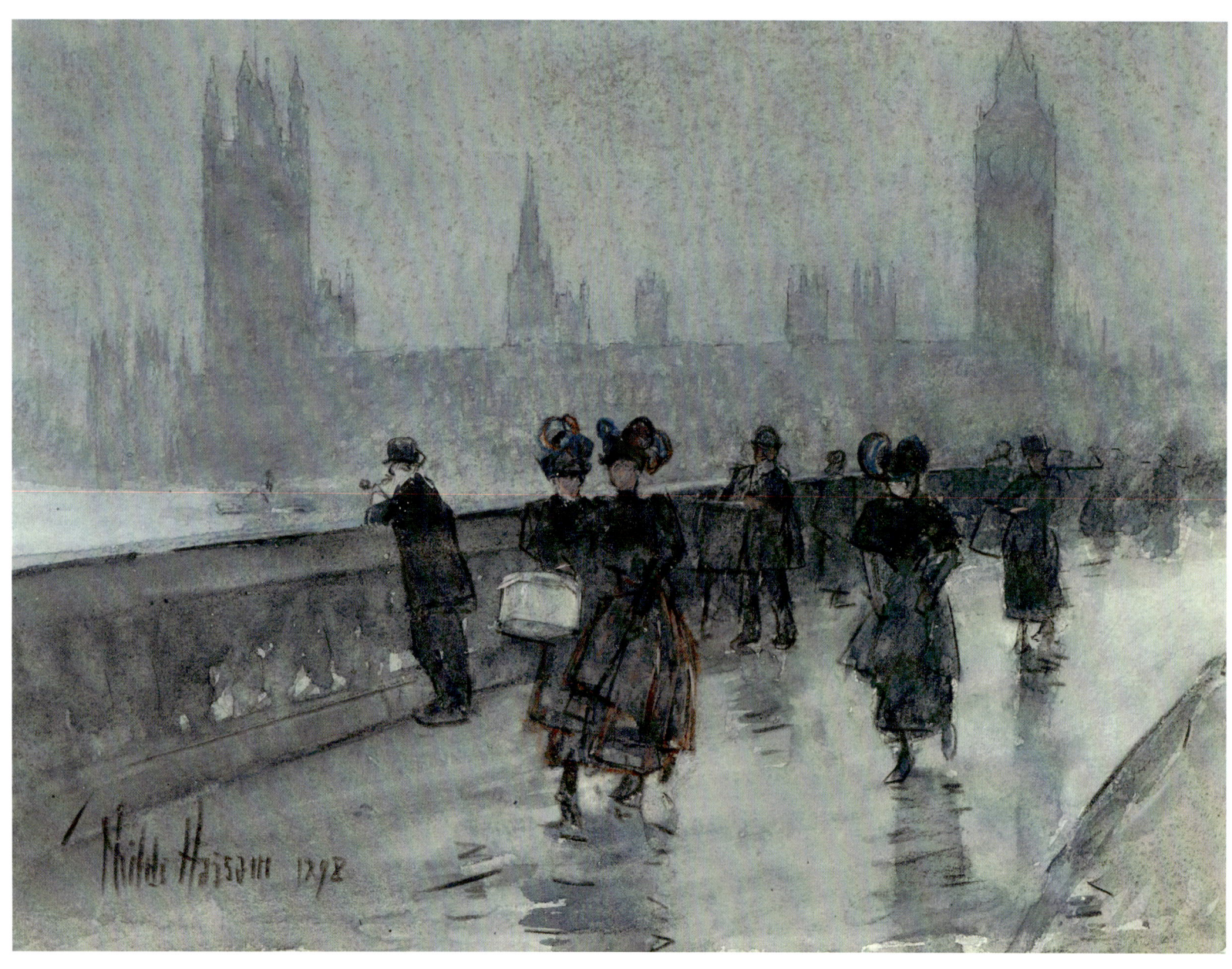

CHILDE HASSAM (1859–1935), **Westminster Bridge,** 1898, color pencil and watercolor, 9 x 11½ inches

34

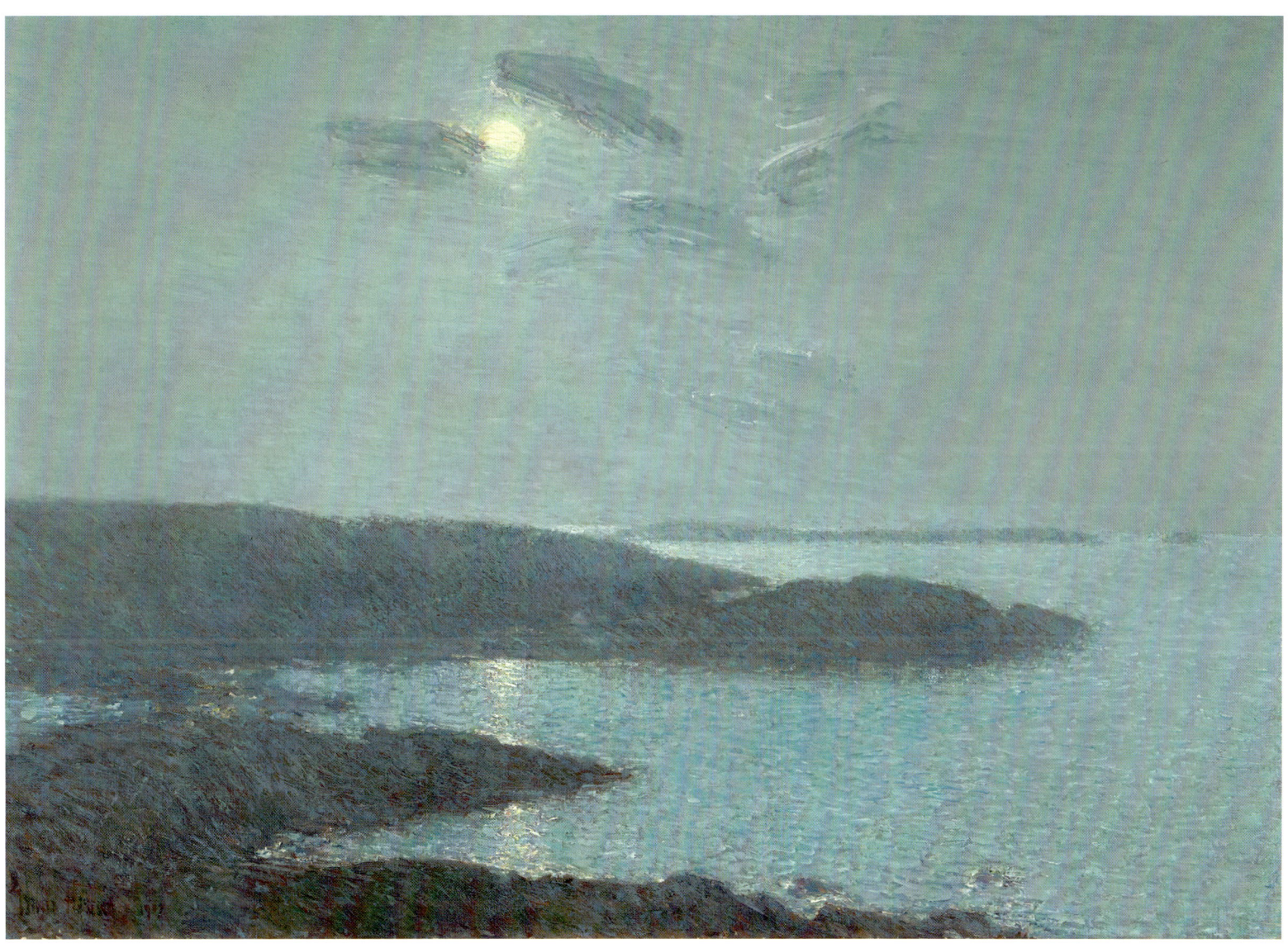

CHILDE HASSAM (1859–1935), **Moonlight, New England Coast,** 1907, oil on canvas, 25 ¾ x 36 ¼ inches

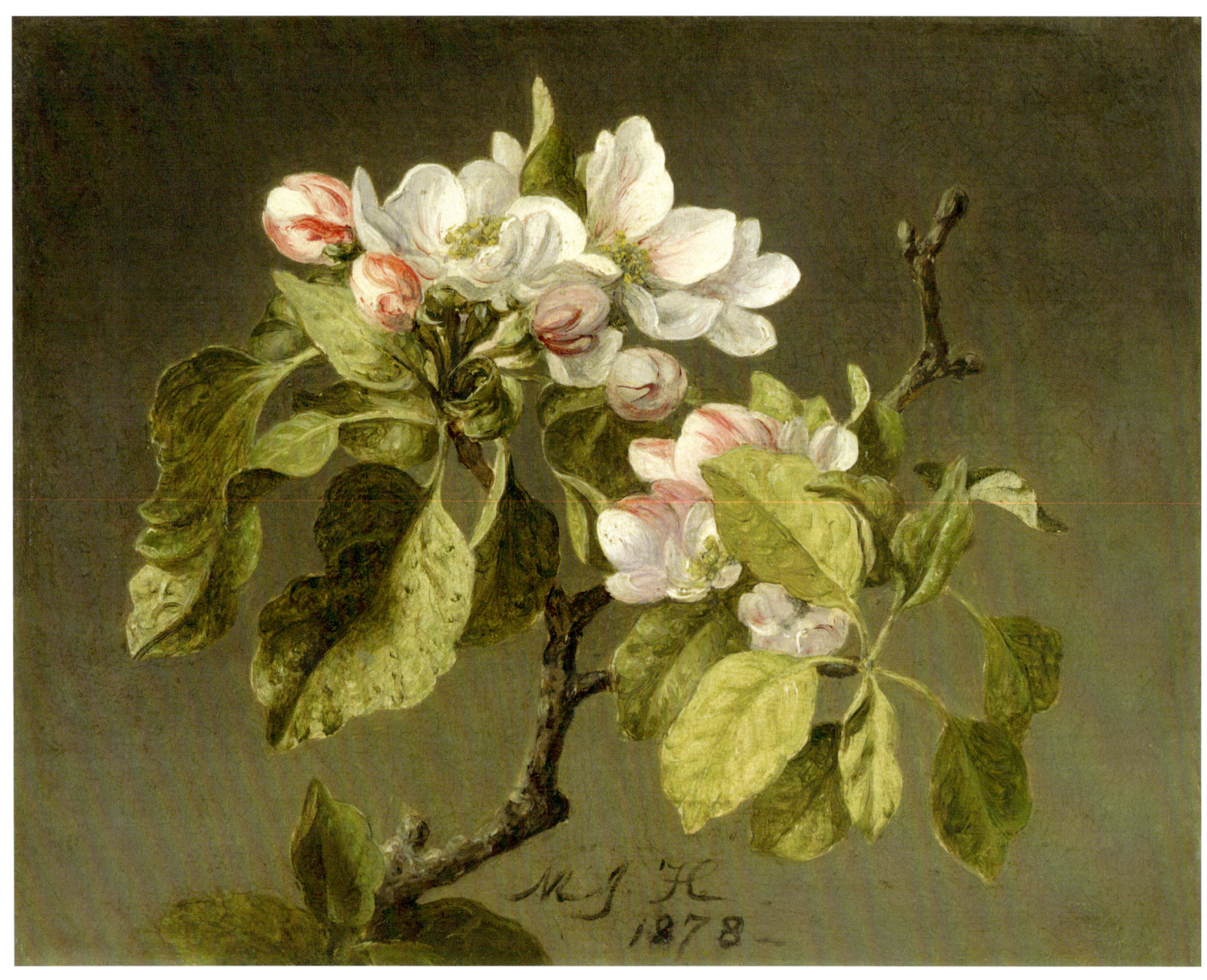

Martin Johnson Heade (1819–1904), **A Branch of Apple Blossoms and Buds,** 1878, oil on canvas, 8 x 10 inches

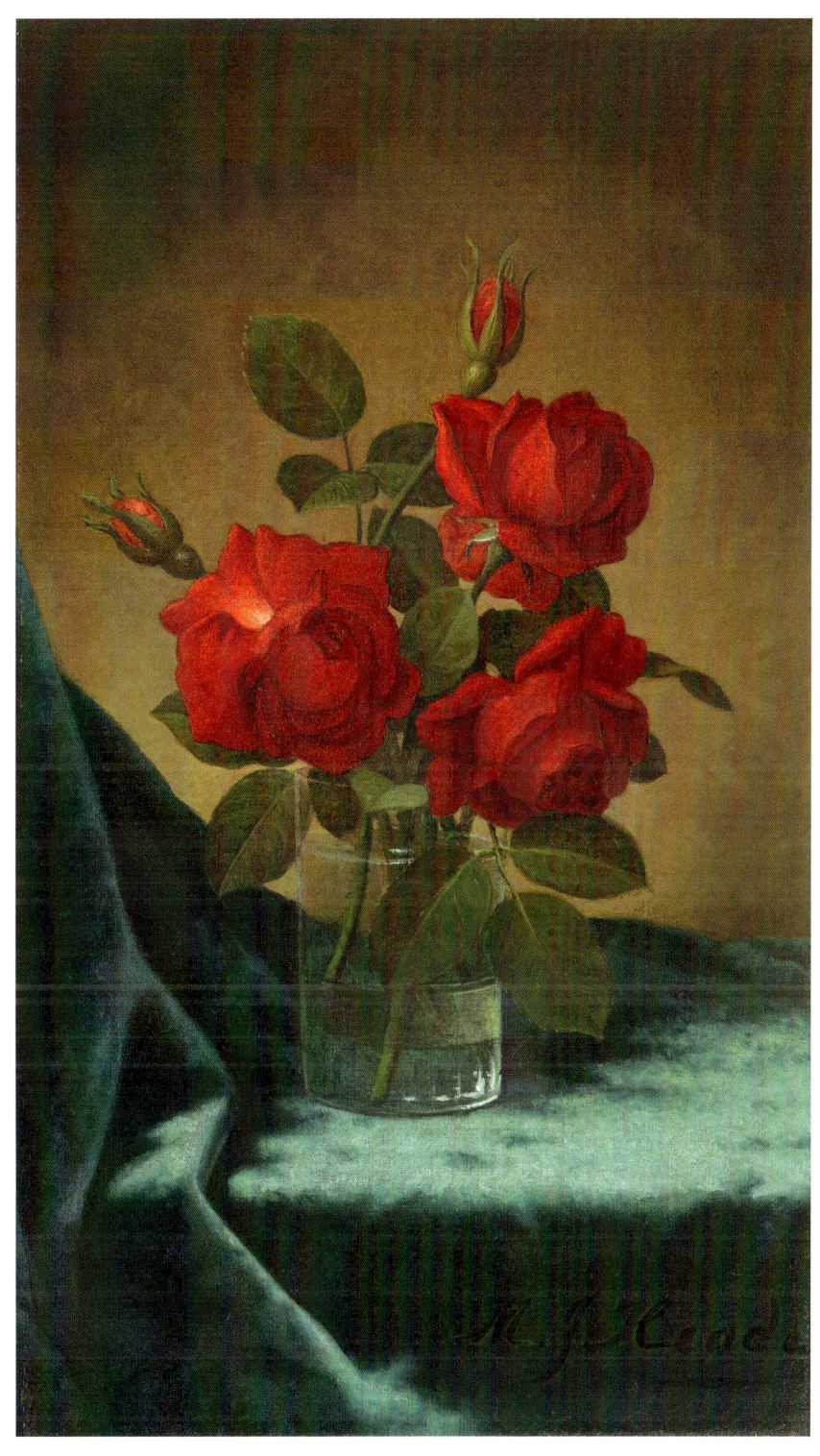

Martin Johnson Heade (1819–1904), **Still Life with Red Roses,** 1880
Oil on canvas, 19 x 11 inches

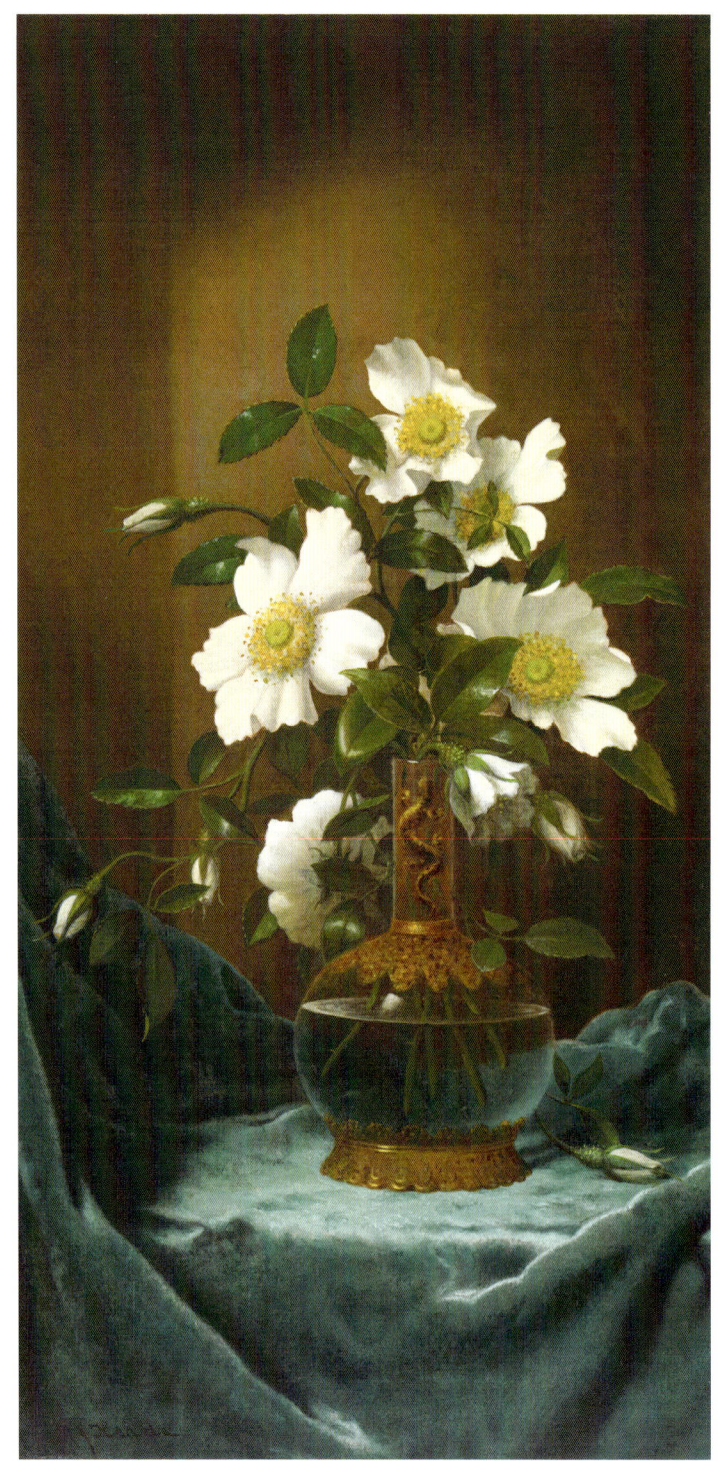

MARTIN JOHNSON HEADE (1819–1904)
White Cherokee Roses in a Salamander Vase, ca. 1883
Oil on canvas, 26 x 13 inches

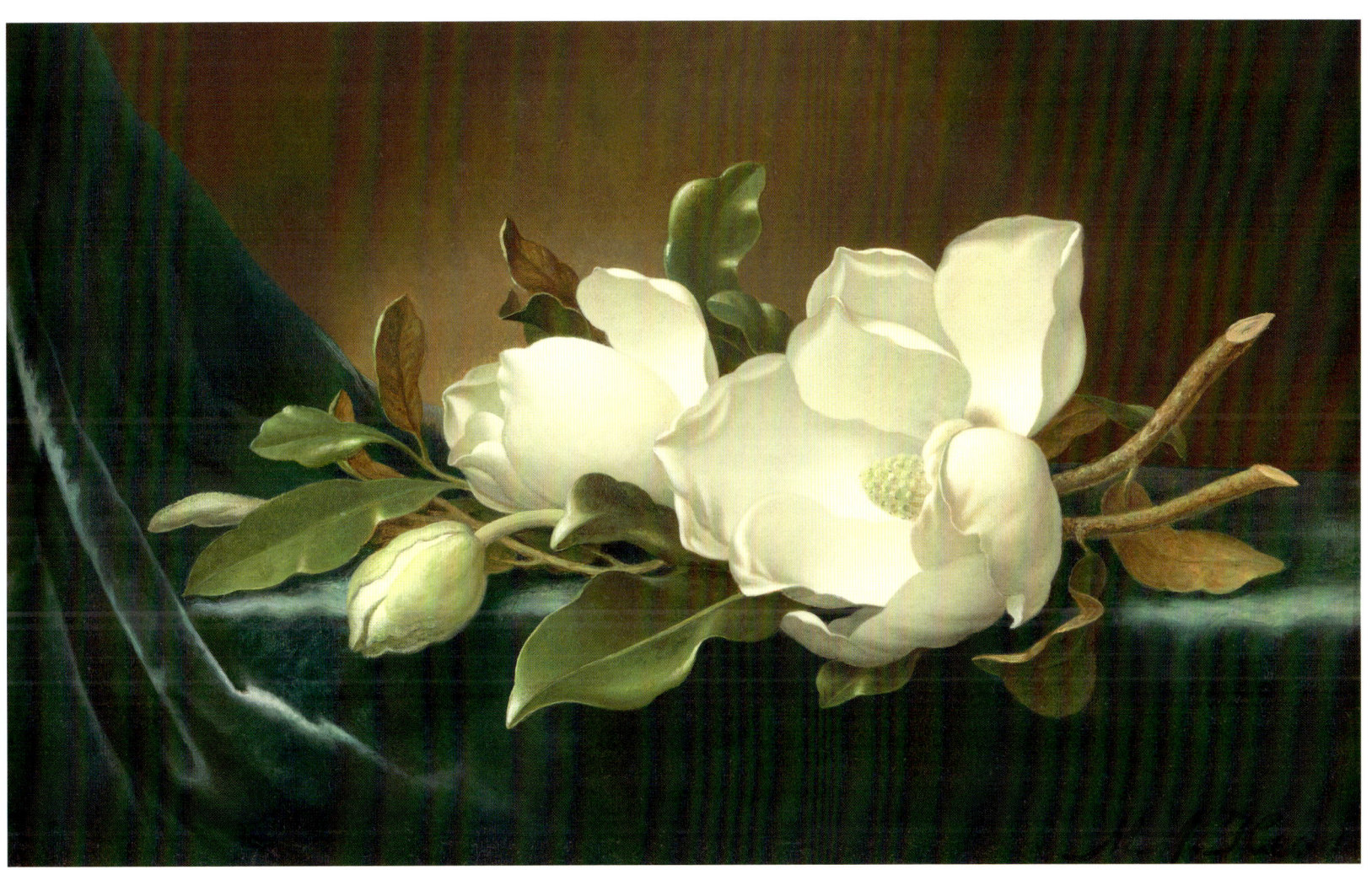

Martin Johnson Heade (1819–1904), **Two Magnolias and a Bud on Teal Velvet,** ca. 1885, oil on canvas, 15 x 24 inches

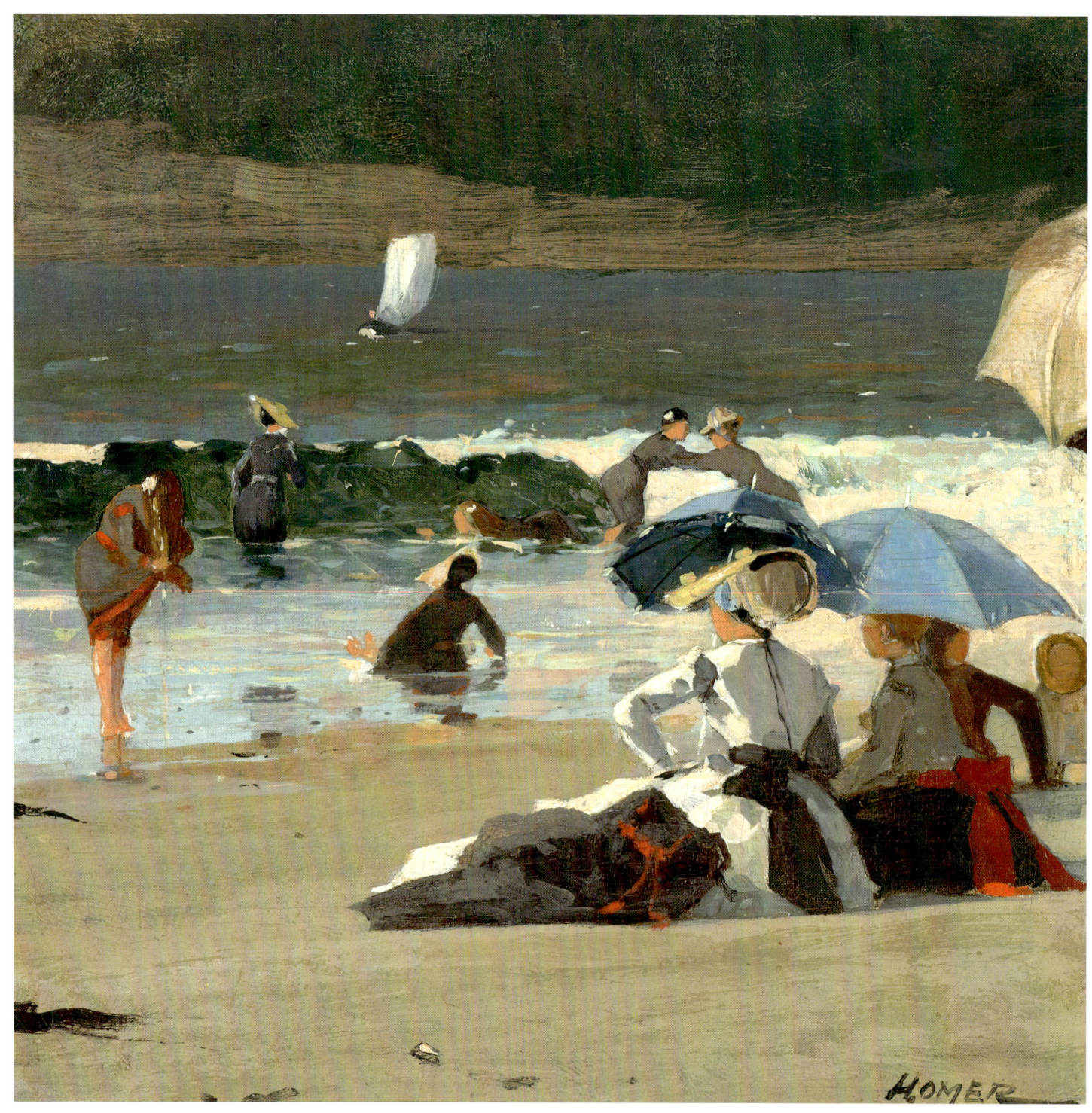

WINSLOW HOMER (1836–1910), **By the Shore,** 1870s, oil on canvas, 9 ½ x 10 inches

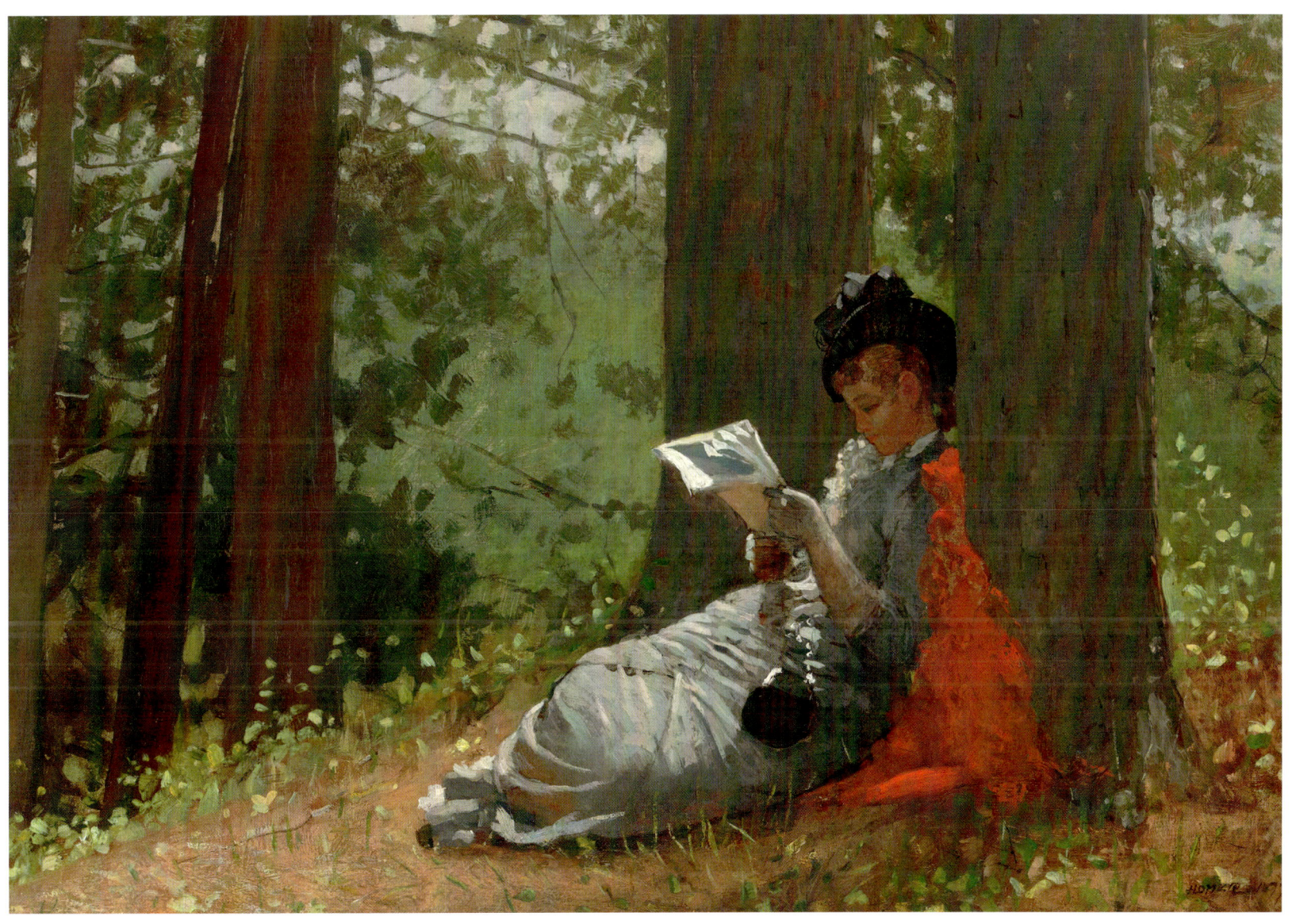

WINSLOW HOMER (1836–1910), **Girl Reading under an Oak Tree,** 1879, oil on canvas, 15 ½ x 22 ½ inches

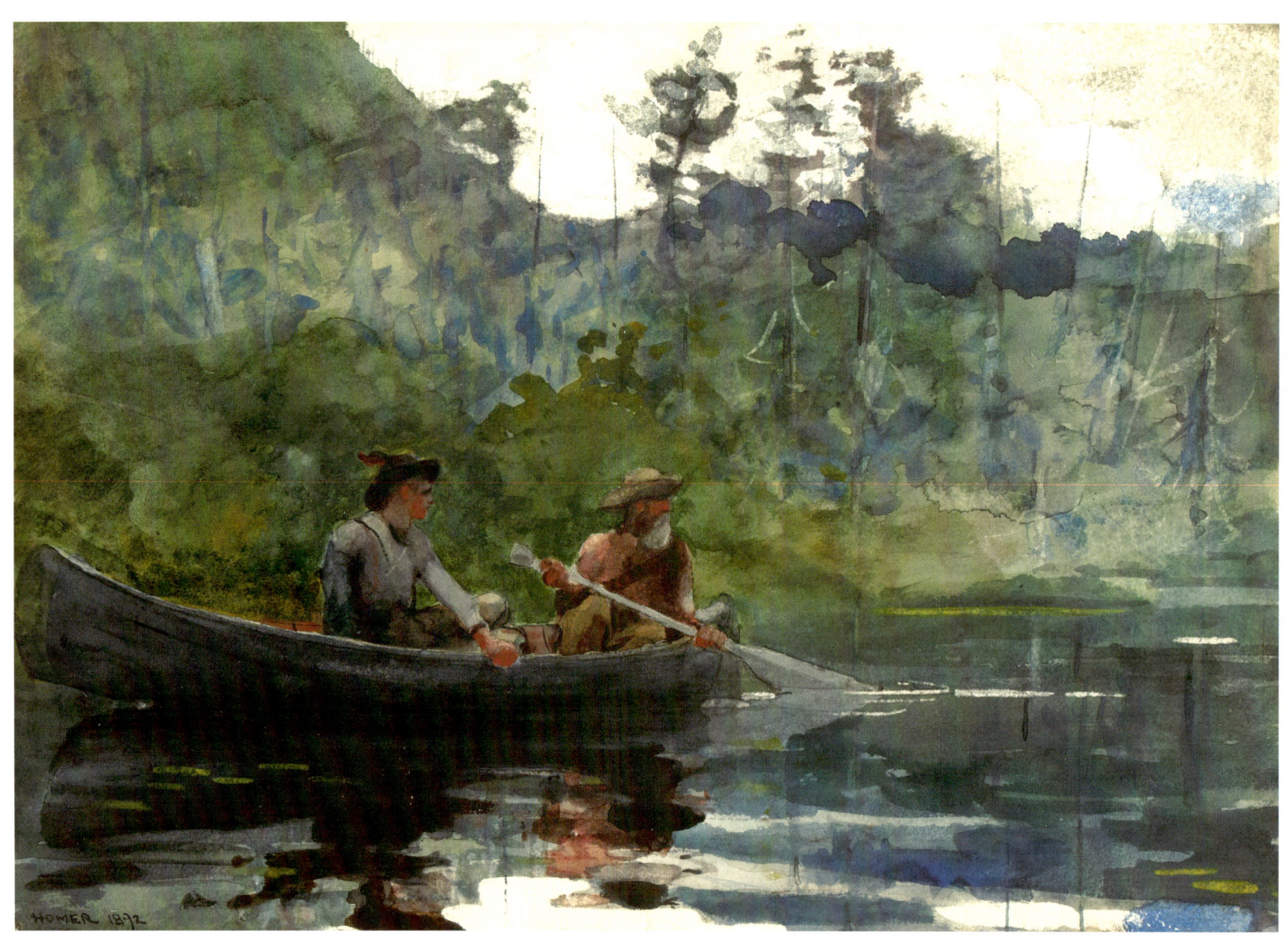

WINSLOW HOMER (1836–1910), **Canoeing in the Adirondacks,** 1892, watercolor over graphite on paper, 15 ½ x 20 inches

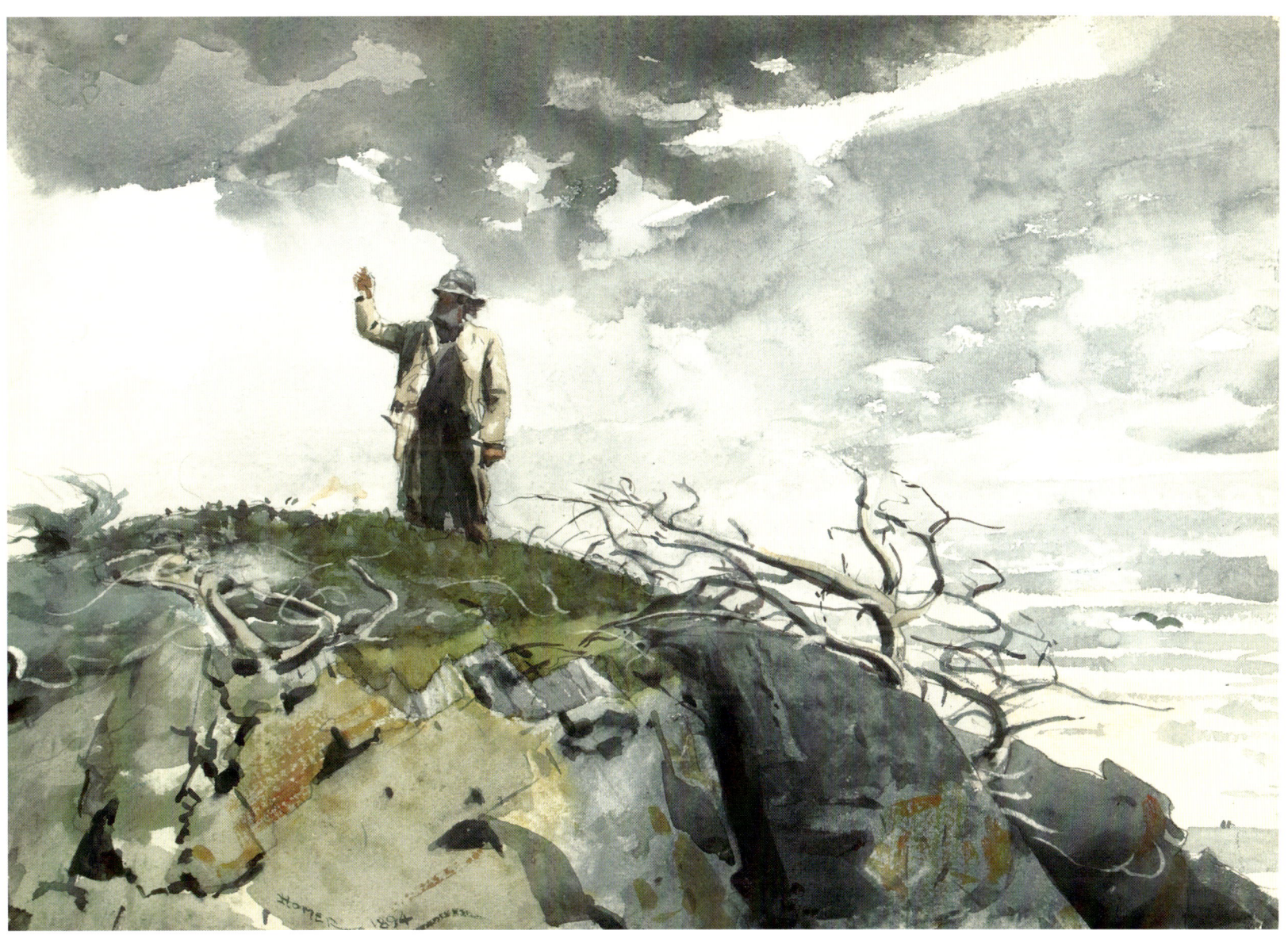

WINSLOW HOMER (1836–1910), **The Watch, Eastern Shore, Prout's Neck,** 1894, watercolor over graphite on paper, 15 ½ x 20 inches

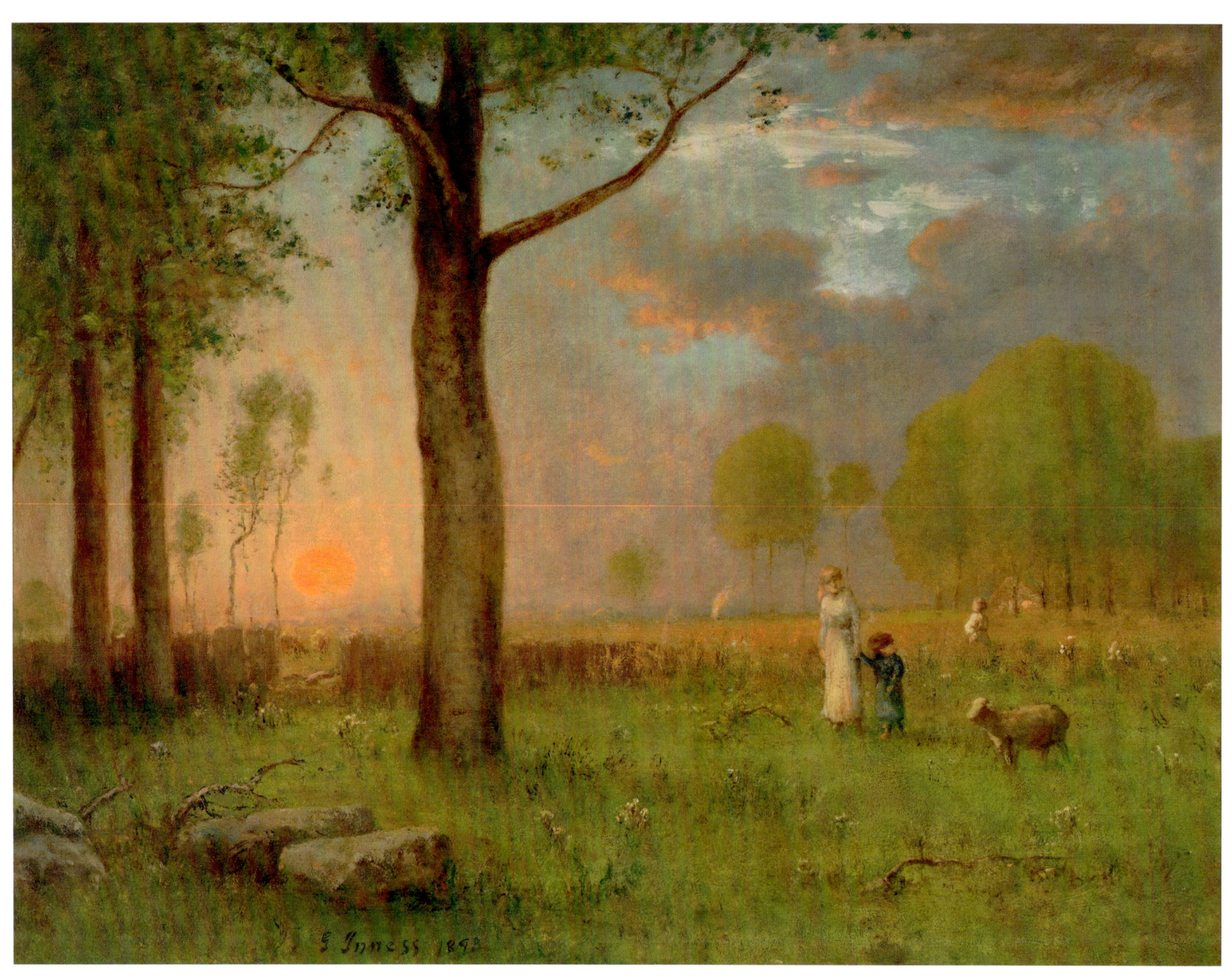

George Inness (1825–1894), **Sunset,** 1893, oil on canvas, 32 ¼ x 42 inches

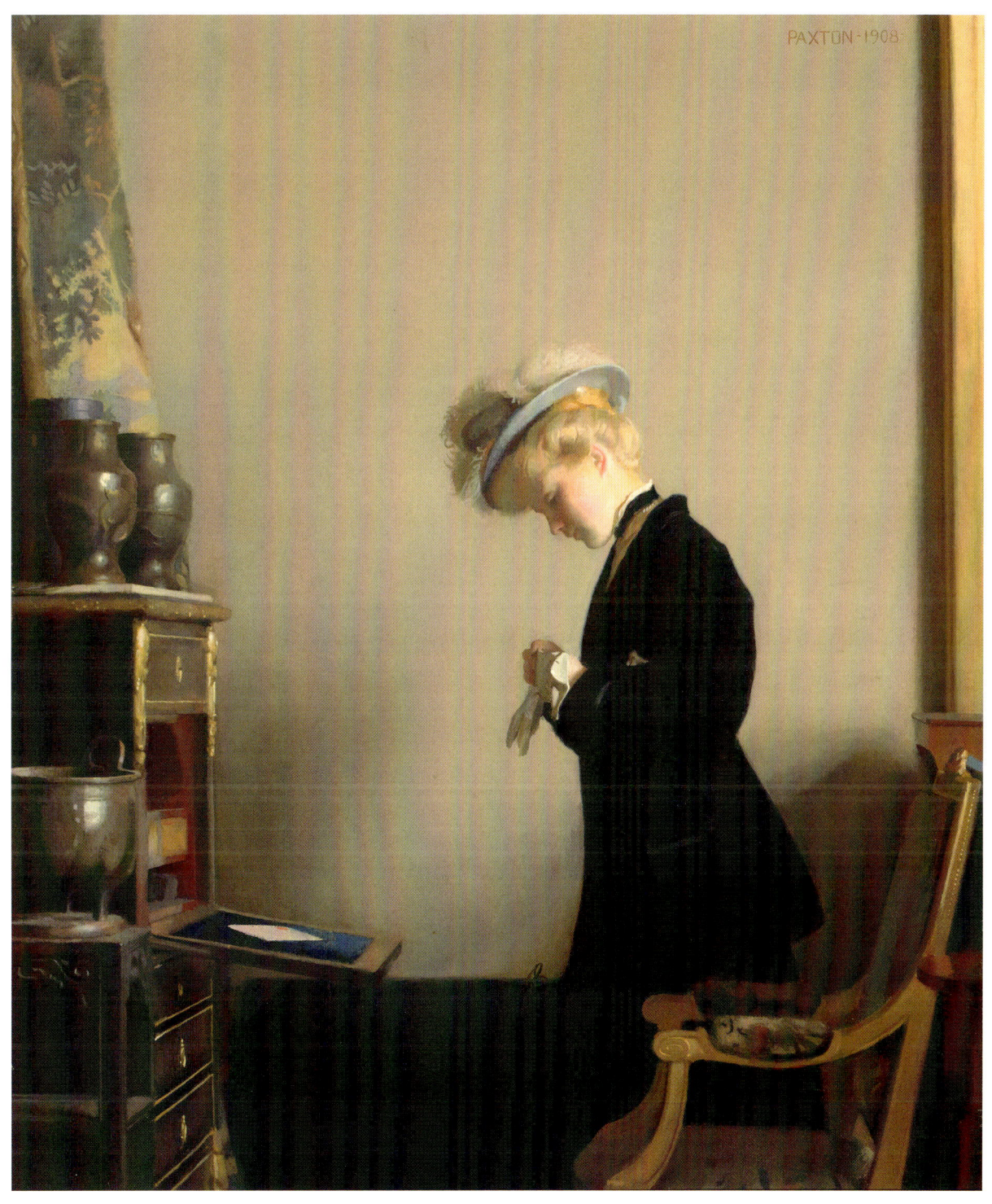

WILLIAM McGREGOR PAXTON (1869–1941), **The Letter,** 1908, oil on canvas, 30 x 25 inches

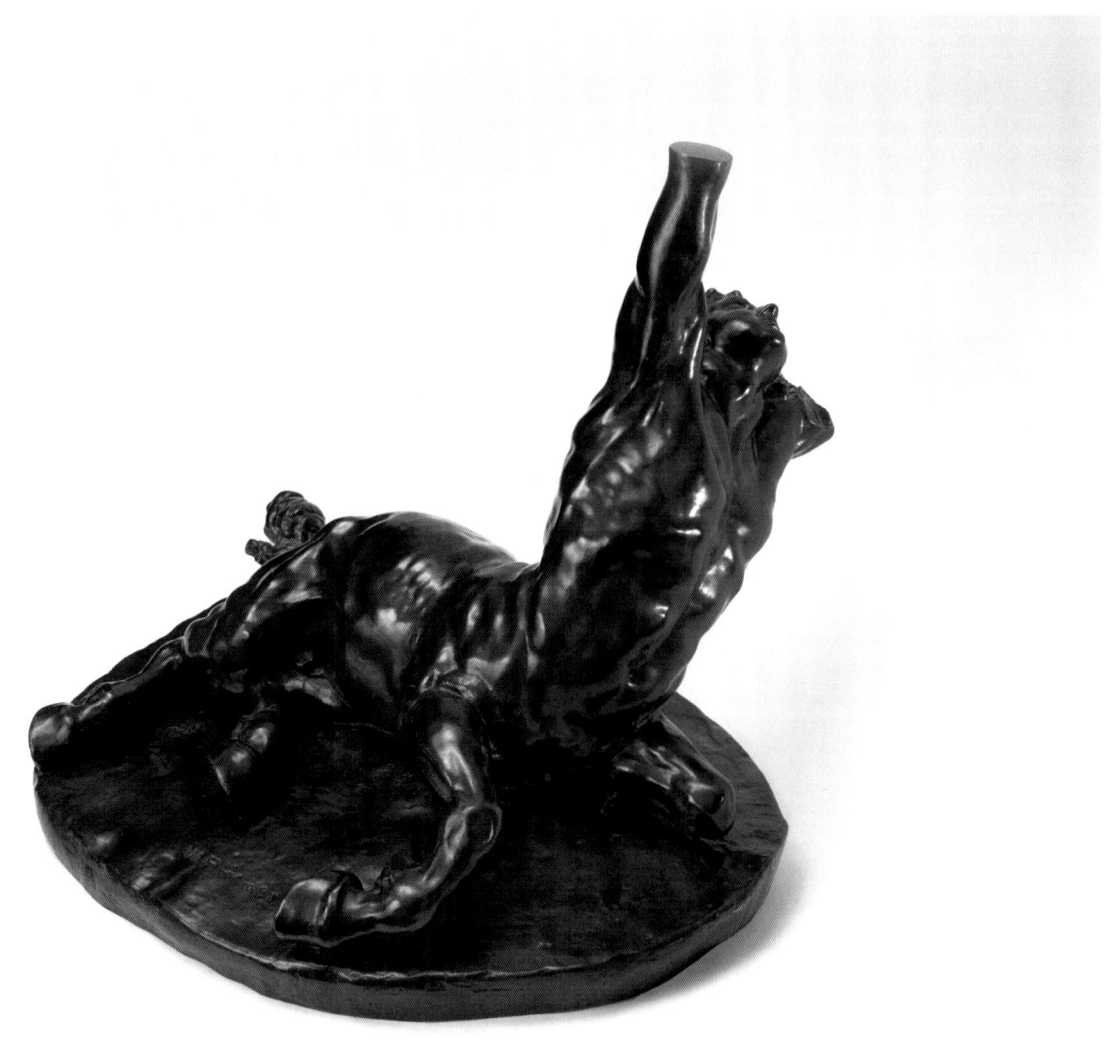

William Rimmer (1816–1879), **The Dying Centaur,** ca. 1890–95, bronze, 22 x 25 x 19 inches

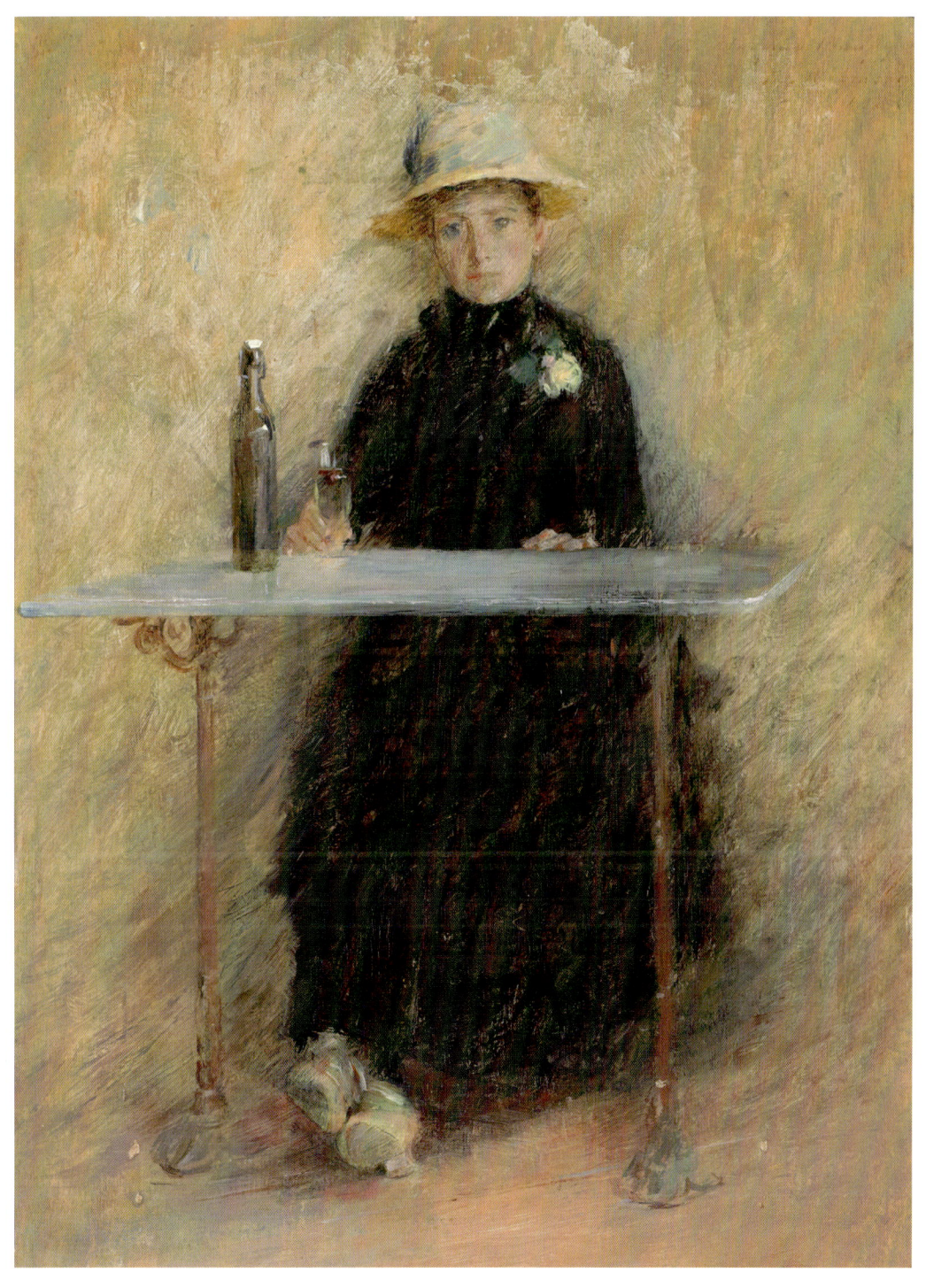

THEODORE ROBINSON (1852–1896), **Portrait of Madame Baudy,** 1888
Oil on canvas, 13 x 9 ½ inches

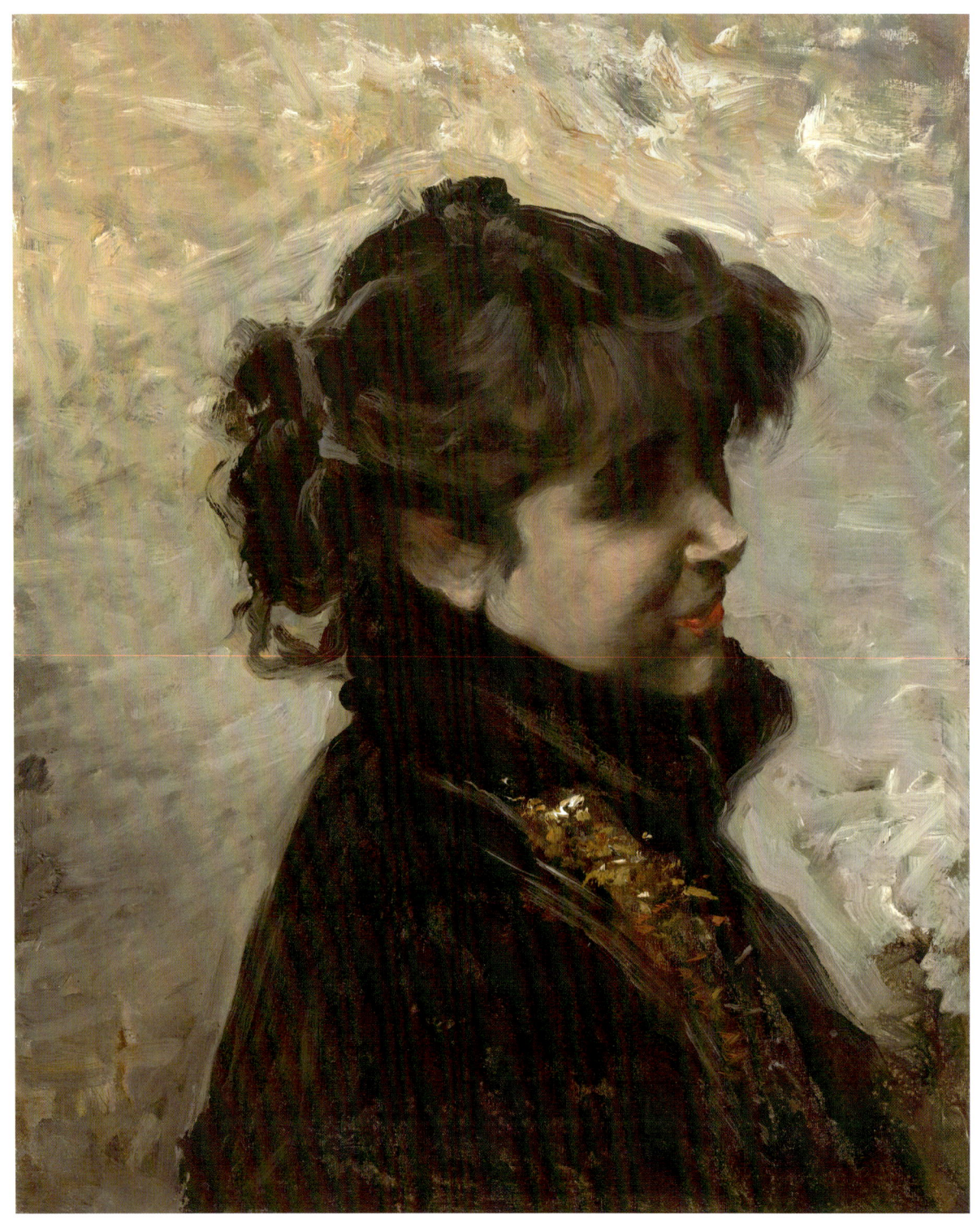

John Singer Sargent (1856–1925), **Madame Errazuriz,** ca. 1883–84, oil on canvas, 18¾ x 15½ inches

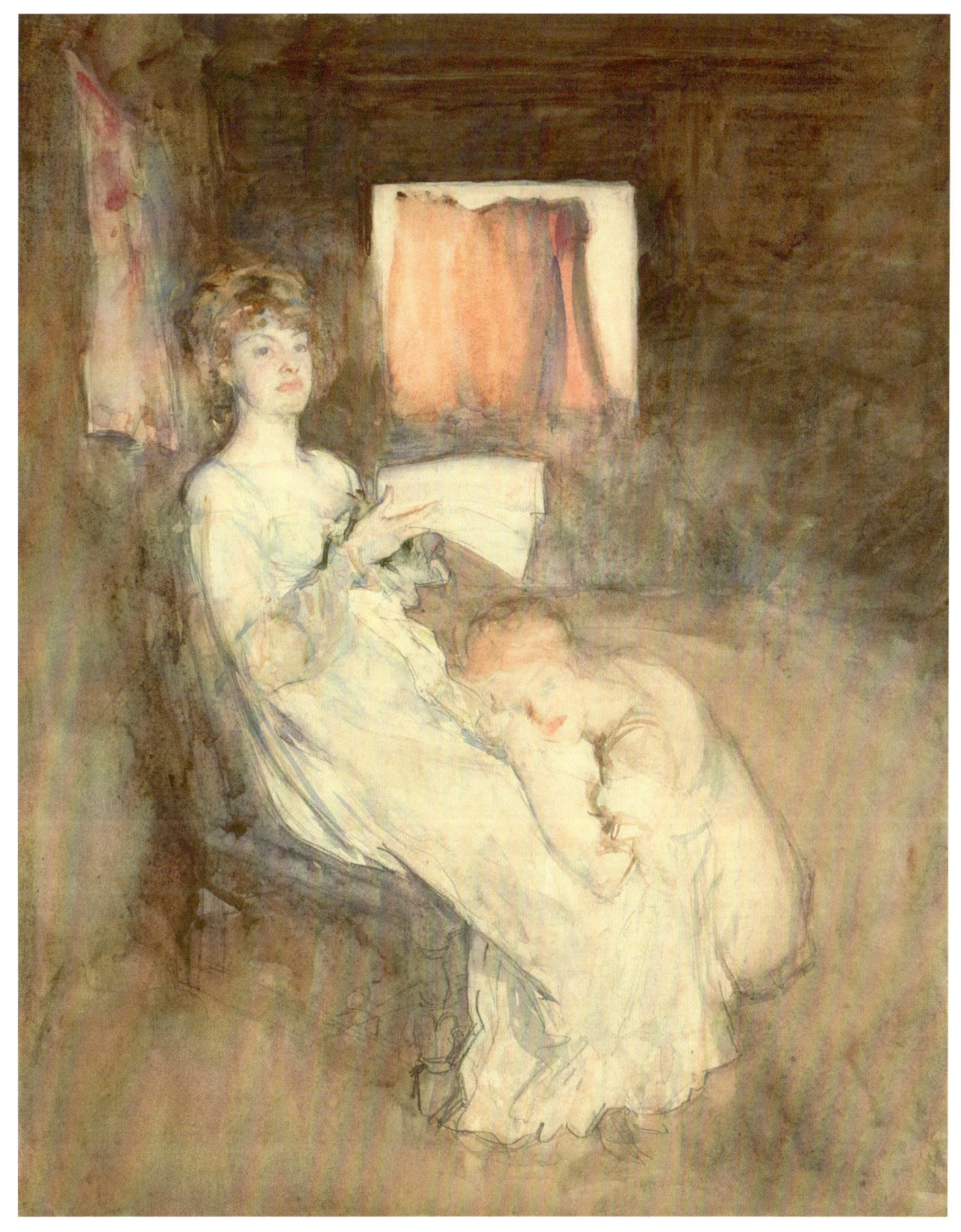

John Singer Sargent (1856 – 1925), **Two Girls,** 1885 – 86,
Watercolor and graphite on paper, 17 ¾ x 13 ⅞ inches

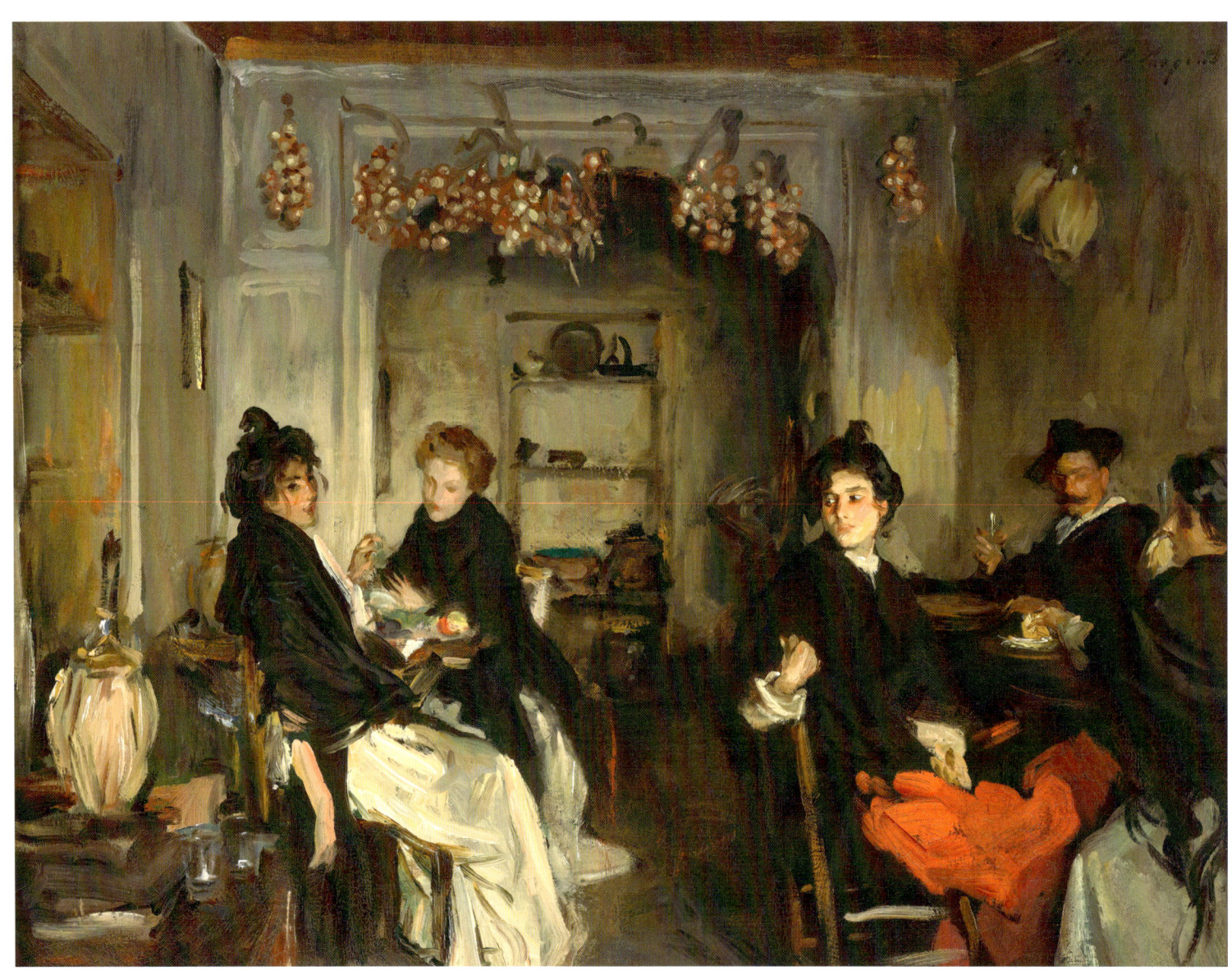

John Singer Sargent (1856–1925), **Venetian Wineshop,** ca. 1898, oil on canvas, 21 x 27 ½ inches

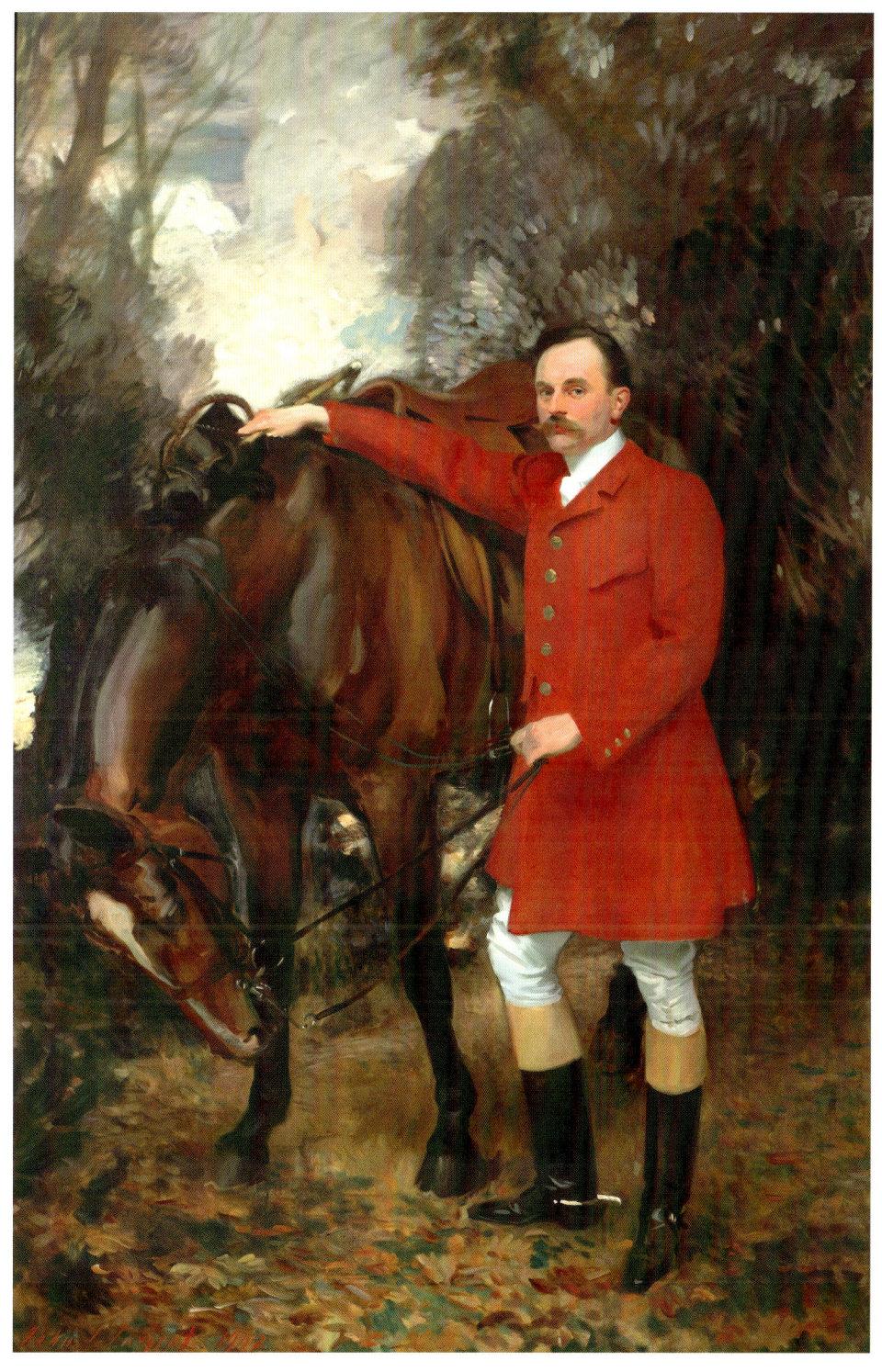

John Singer Sargent (1856–1925), **Portrait of William Marshall Cazalet,** 1902
Oil on canvas, 100 x 65 inches

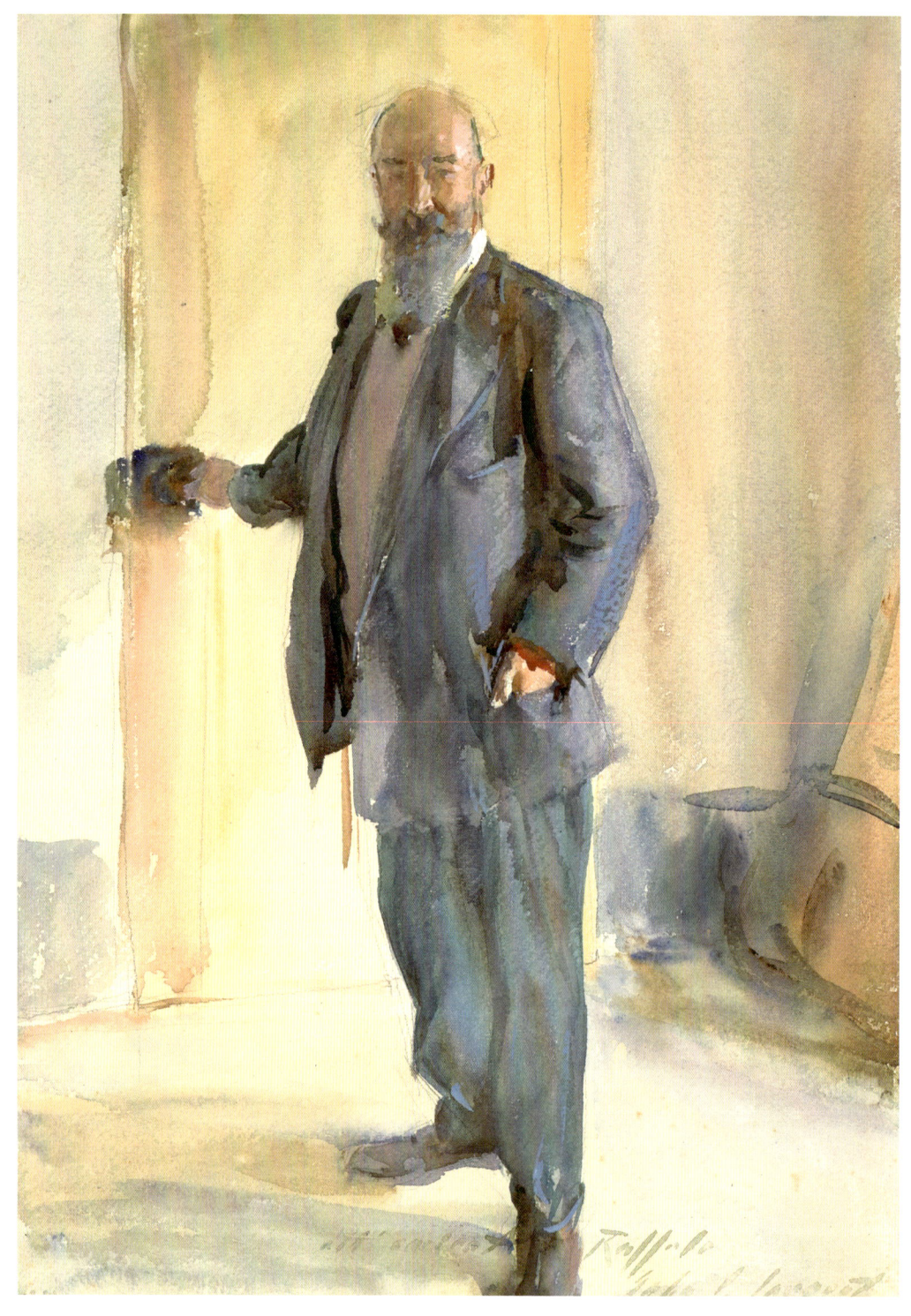

JOHN SINGER SARGENT (1856–1925), **Portrait of Ambrogio Raffele,** 1904–11
Watercolor over graphite on paper, 20 x 14 inches

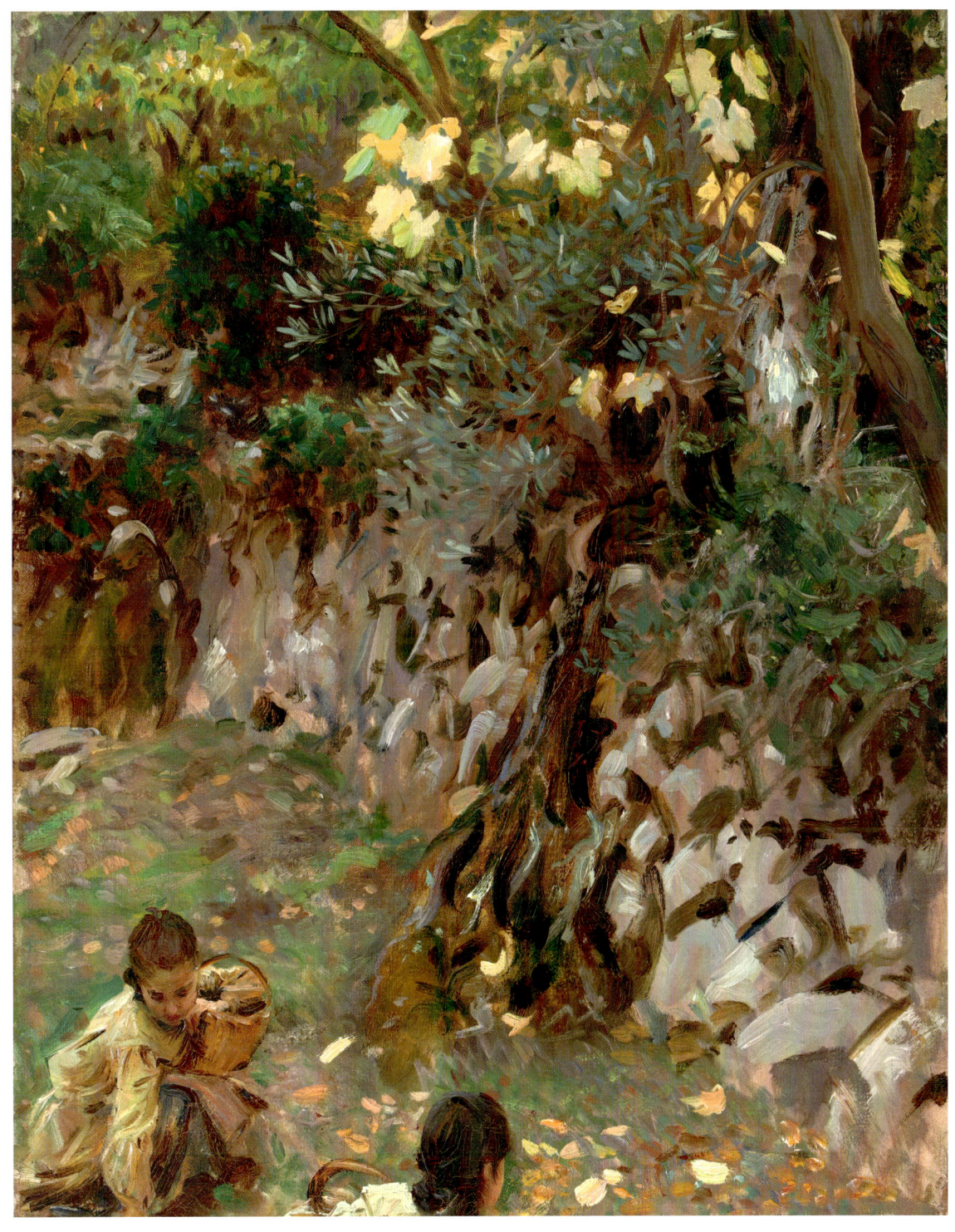

John Singer Sargent (1856–1925), **Gathering Blossoms, Valdemosa,** 1908
Oil on canvas, 28 x 22 inches

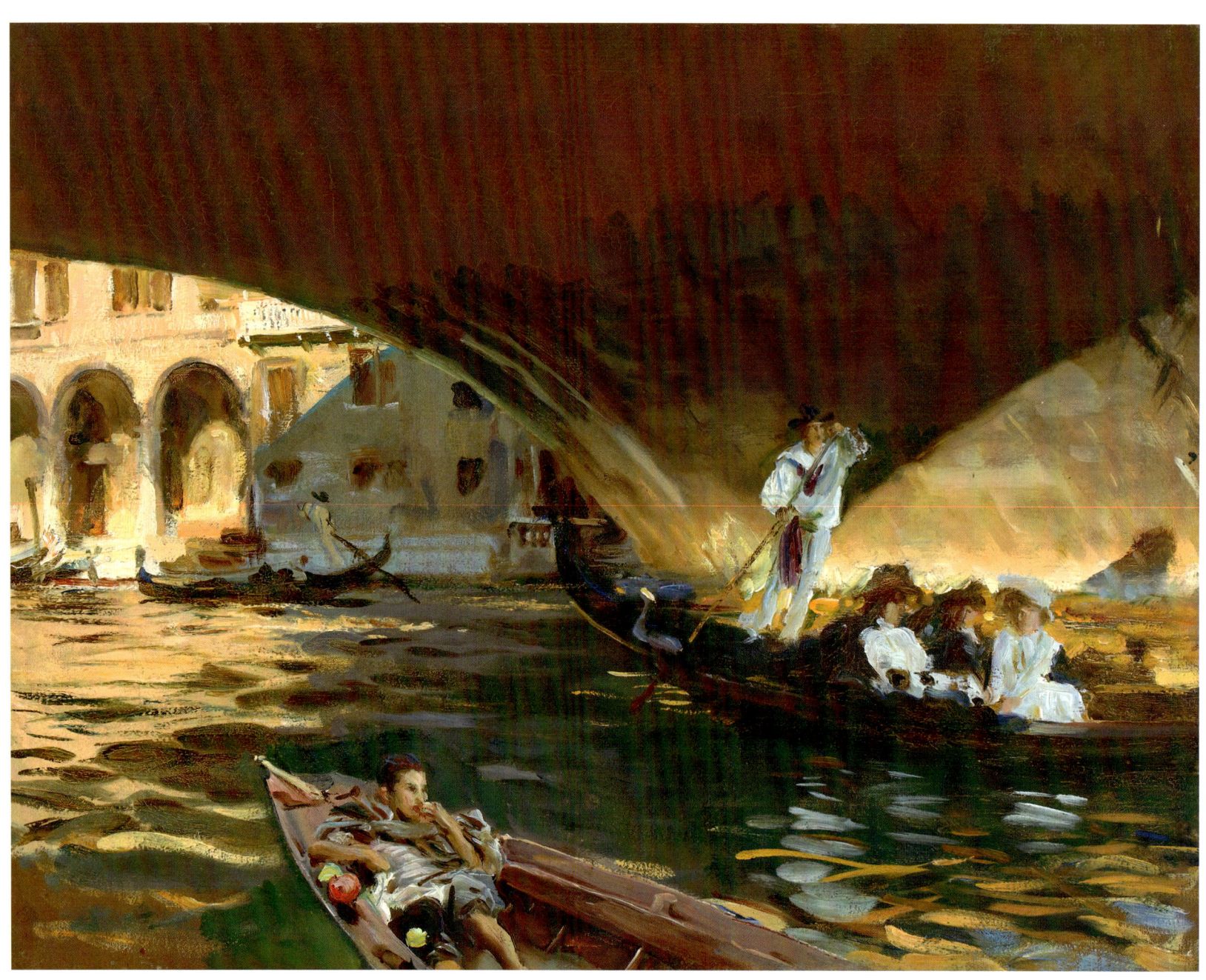

JOHN SINGER SARGENT (1856–1925), **The Rialto,** 1909, oil on canvas, 21 ½ x 26 inches

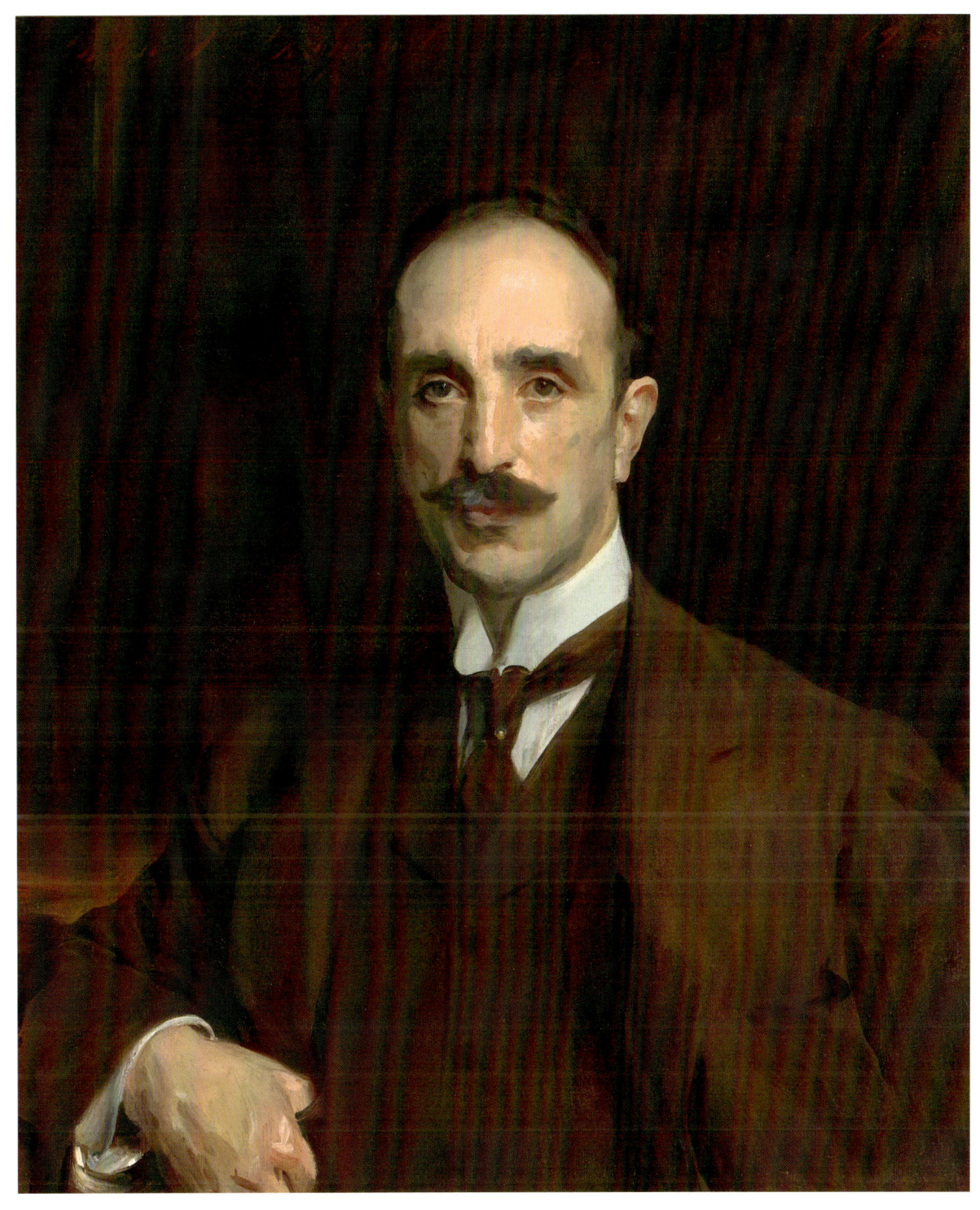

John Singer Sargent (1856–1925), **Portrait of Douglas Vickers,** 1914
oil on canvas, 31 x 25 inches

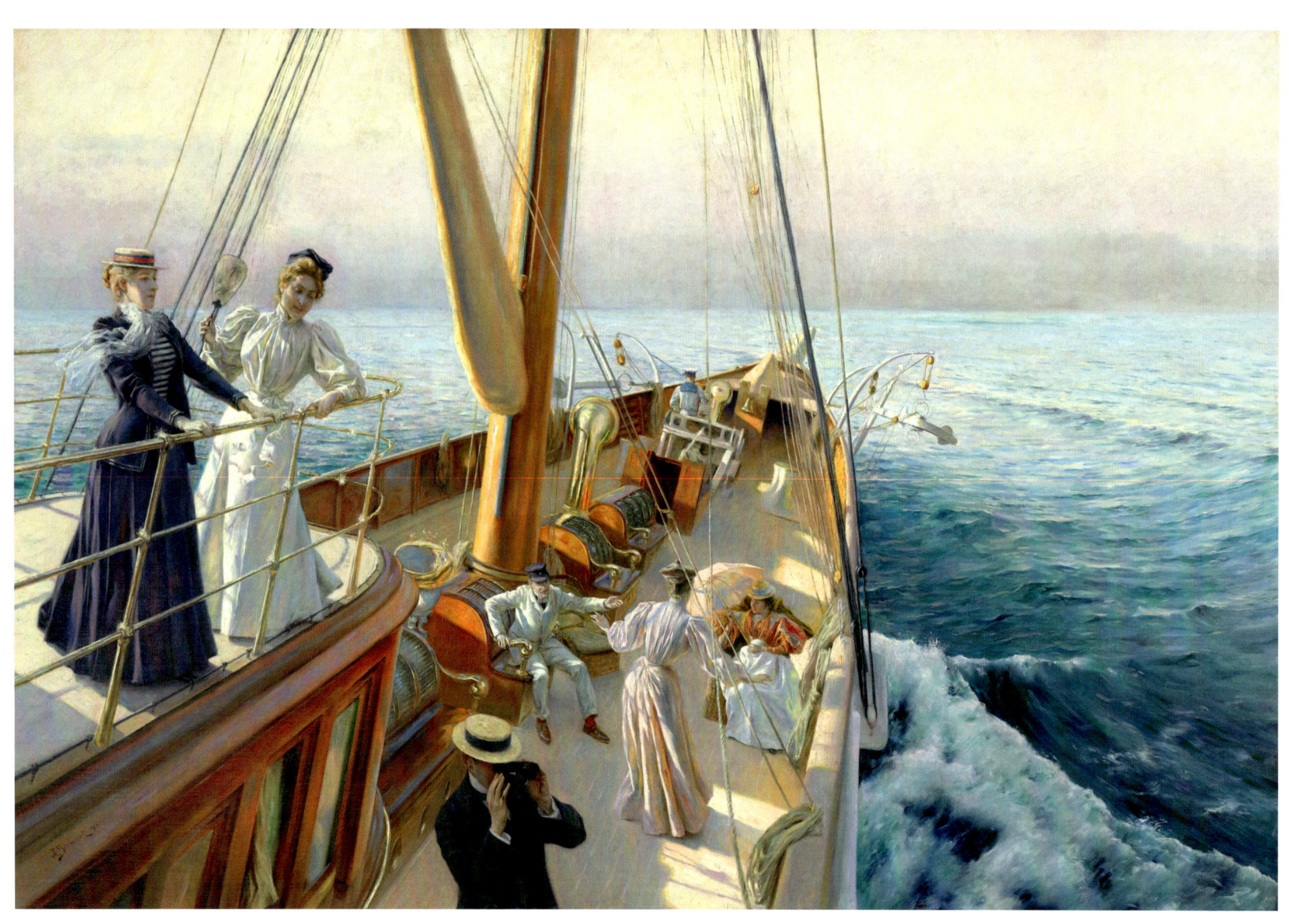

Julius L. Stewart (1855–1919), **Yachting in the Mediterranean**, 1896
Oil on canvas, 43 ½ x 63 ½ inches

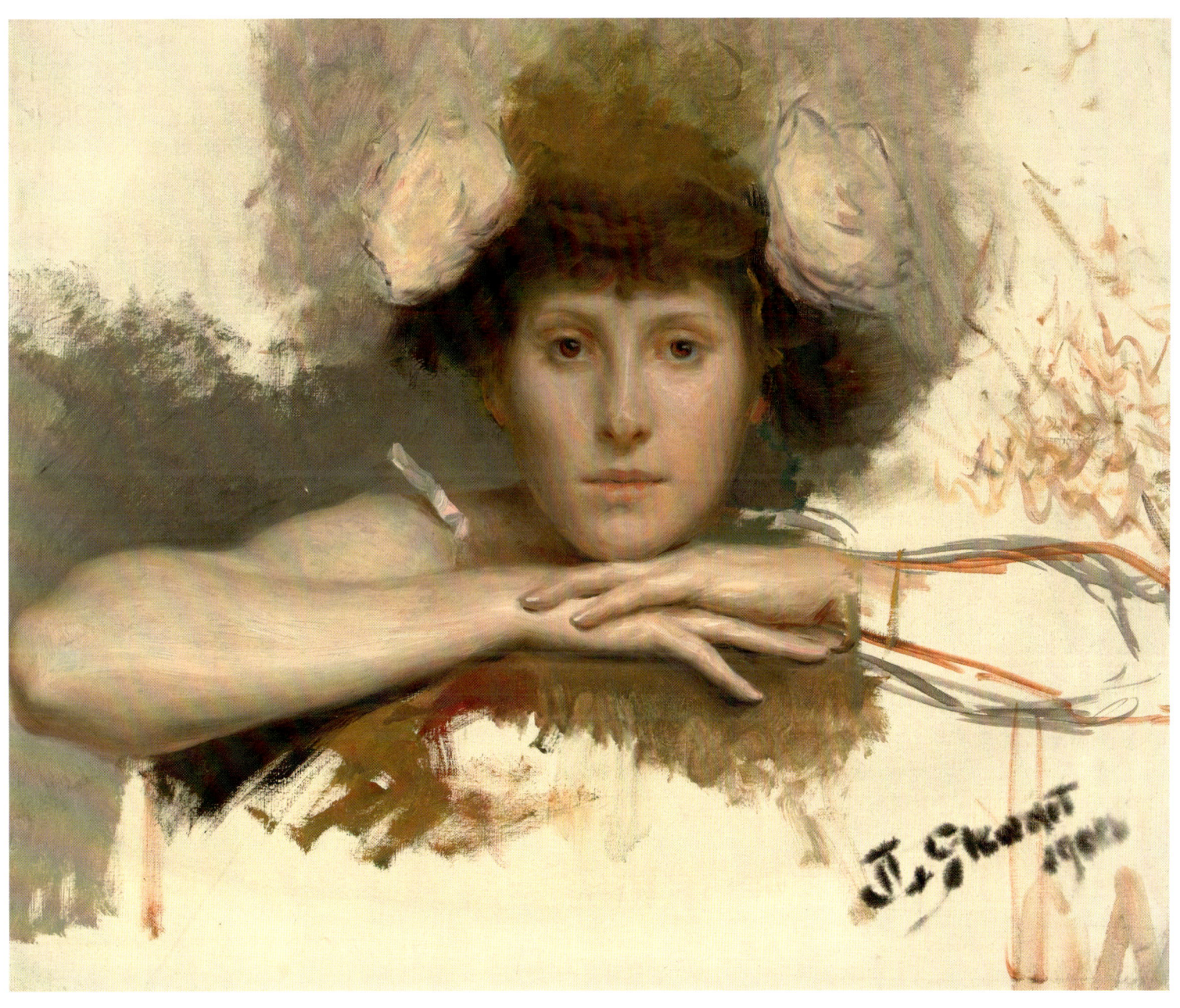

Julius L. Stewart (1855–1919), **Flowers in Her Hair,** 1900, oil on canvas, 19 x 23 ¾ inches

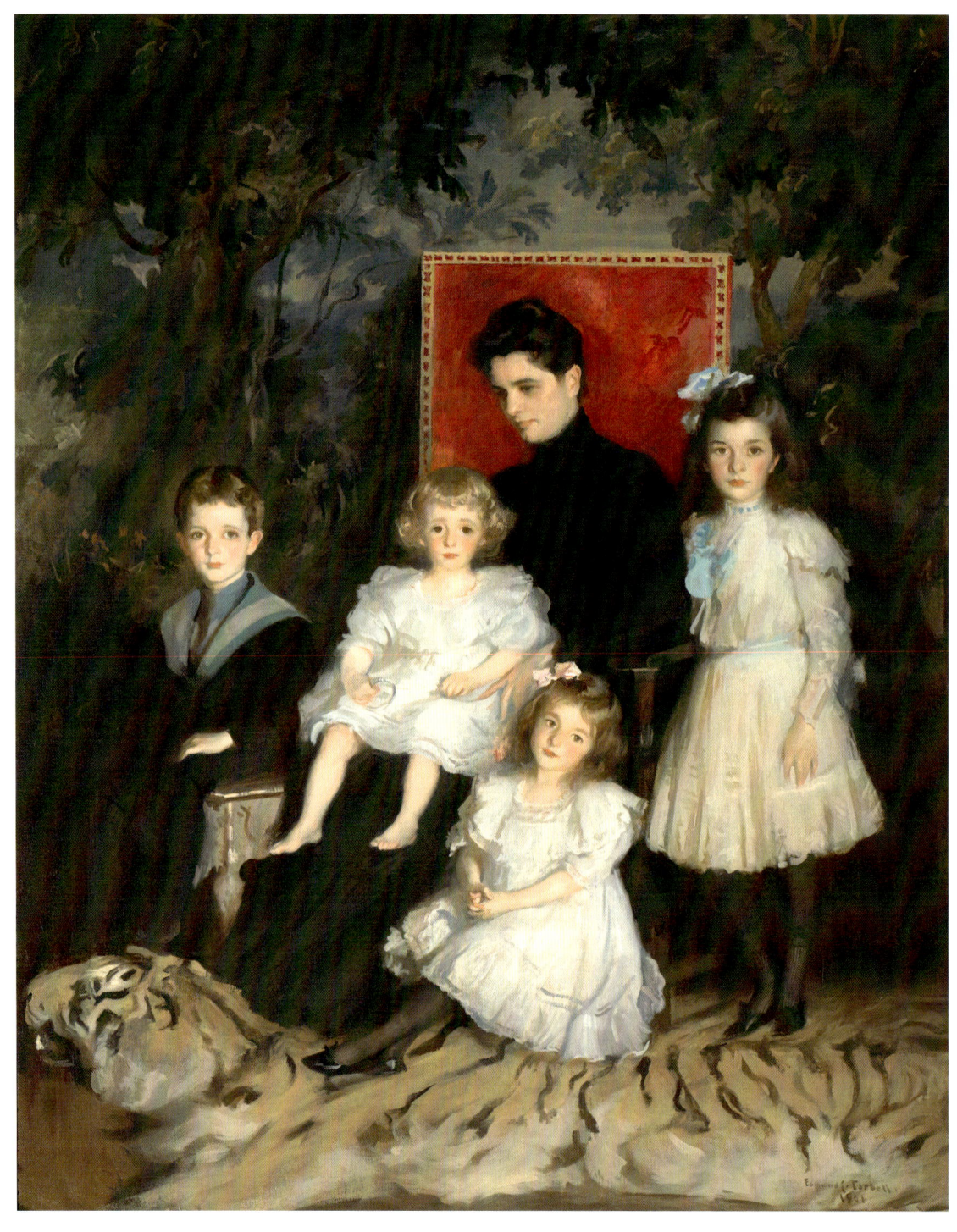

Edmund Tarbell (1862–1938), **Mrs. Horatio Nelson-Slater and Children,** 1901
Oil on canvas, 89 x 69 inches

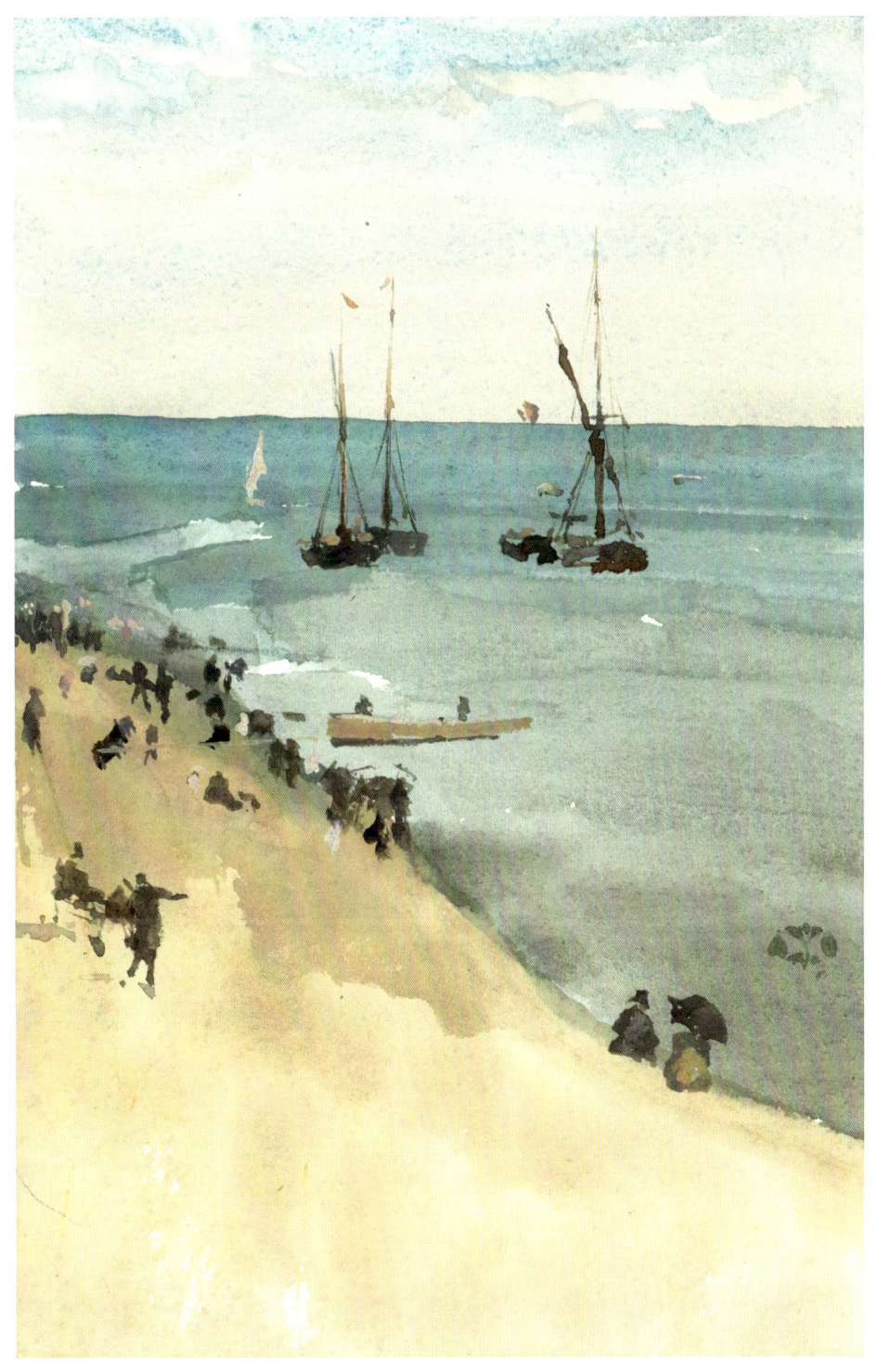

JAMES McNEILL WHISTLER (1834–1903), **Green and Silver—The Bright Sea, Dieppe,** ca. 1883
Watercolor and gouache on paper, 10 x 7 ⅛ inches

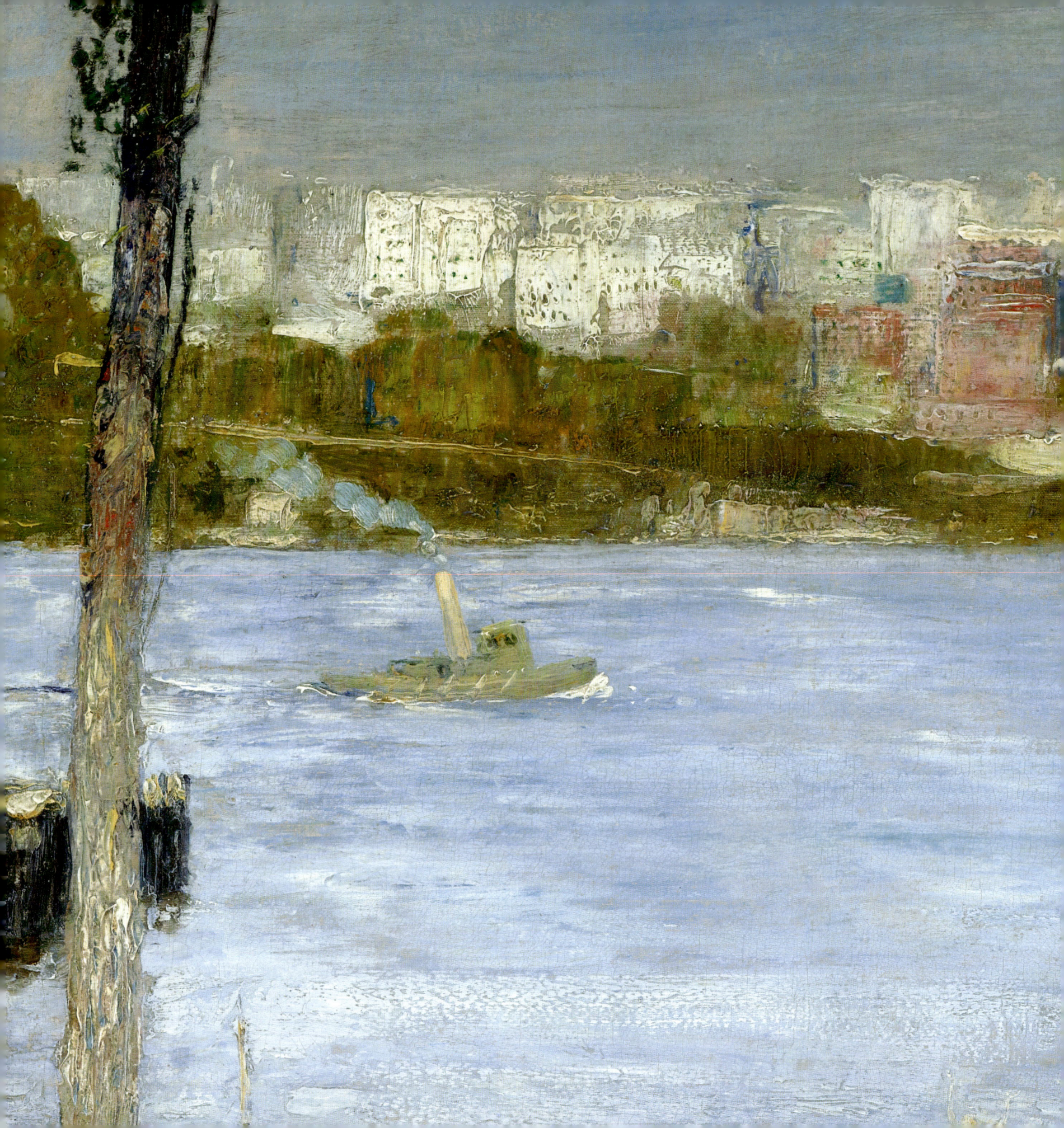

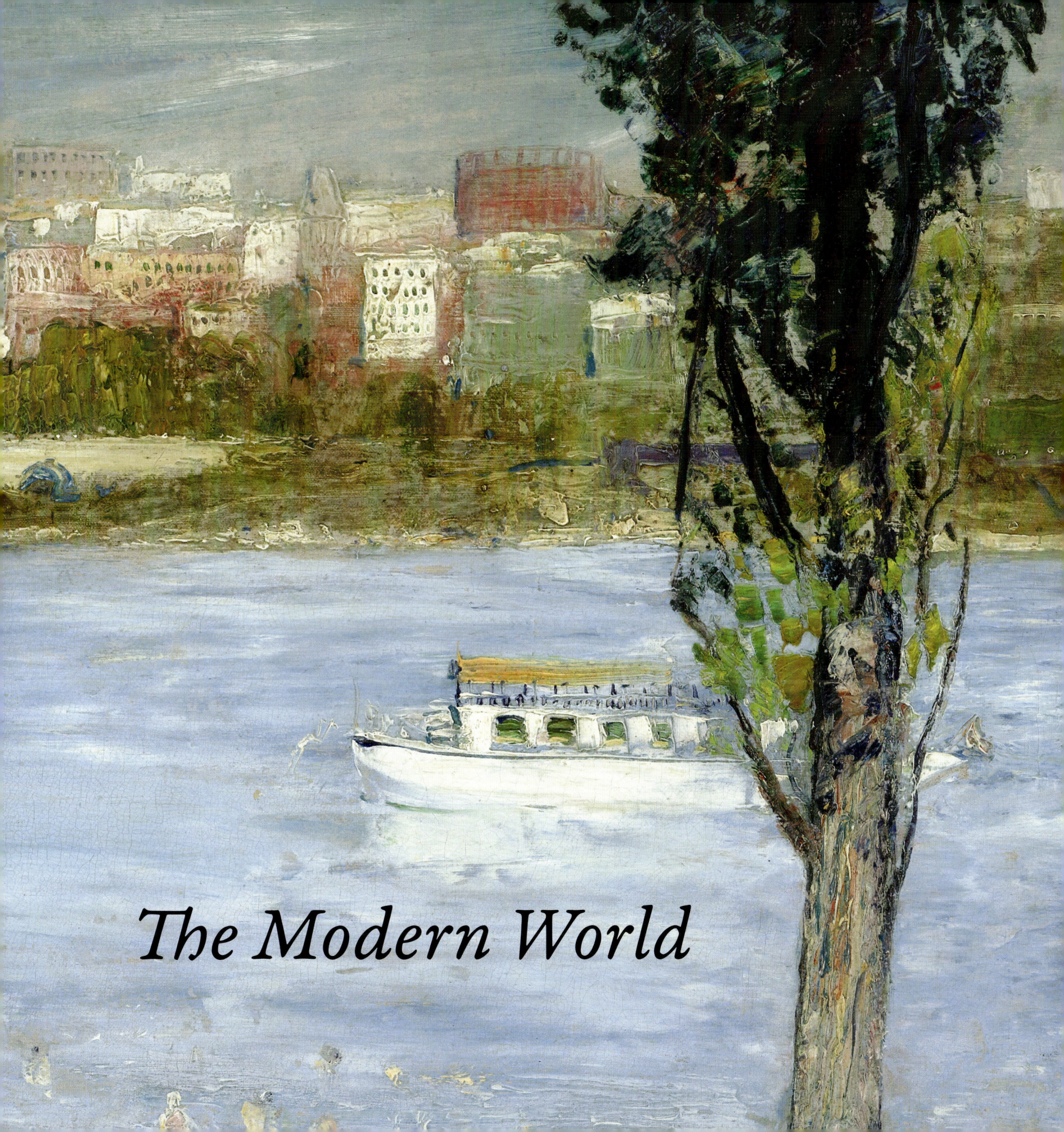

The Modern World

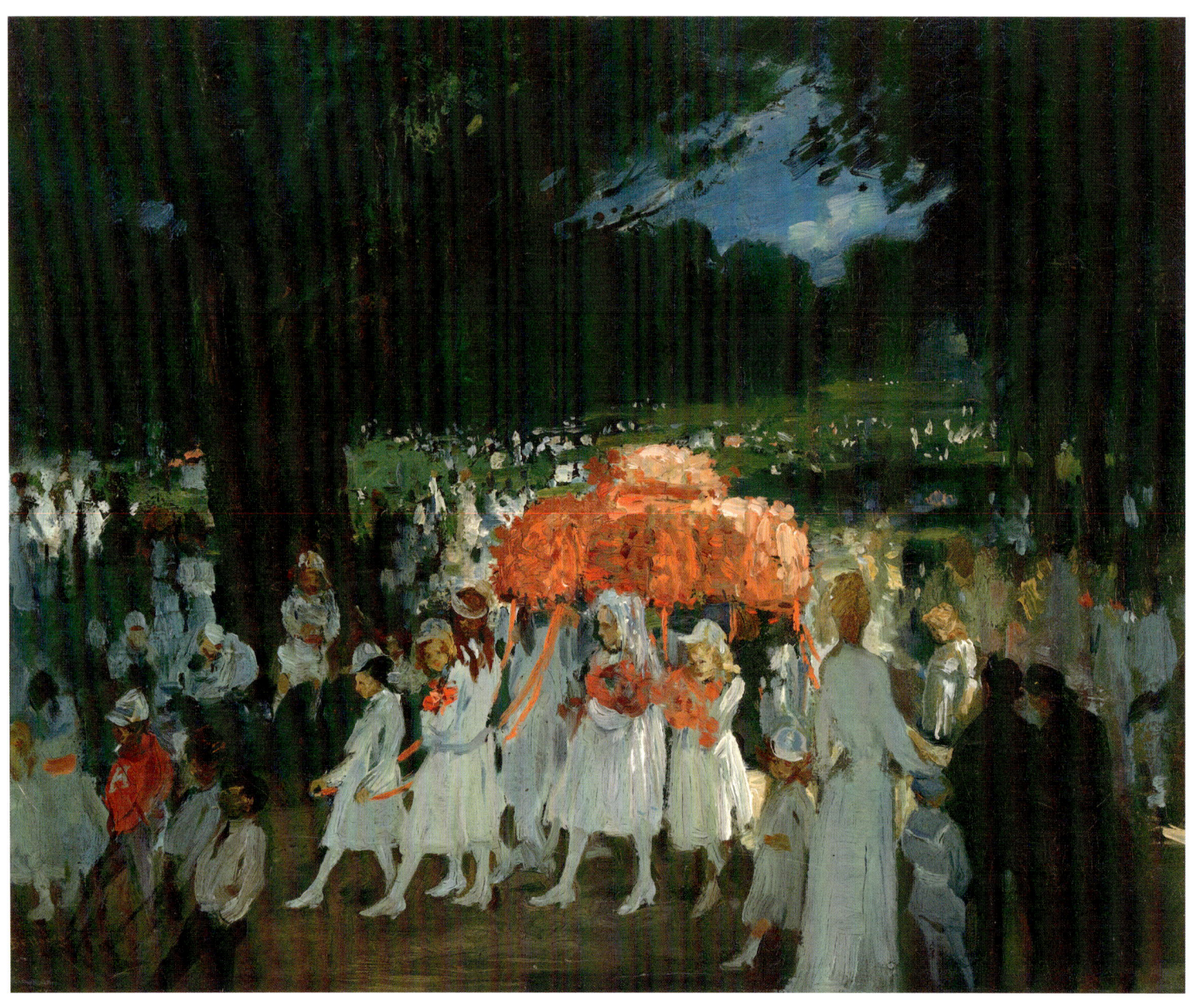

George Bellows (1882–1925), **May Day in Central Park,** ca. 1905, oil on canvas, 18 x 22 inches

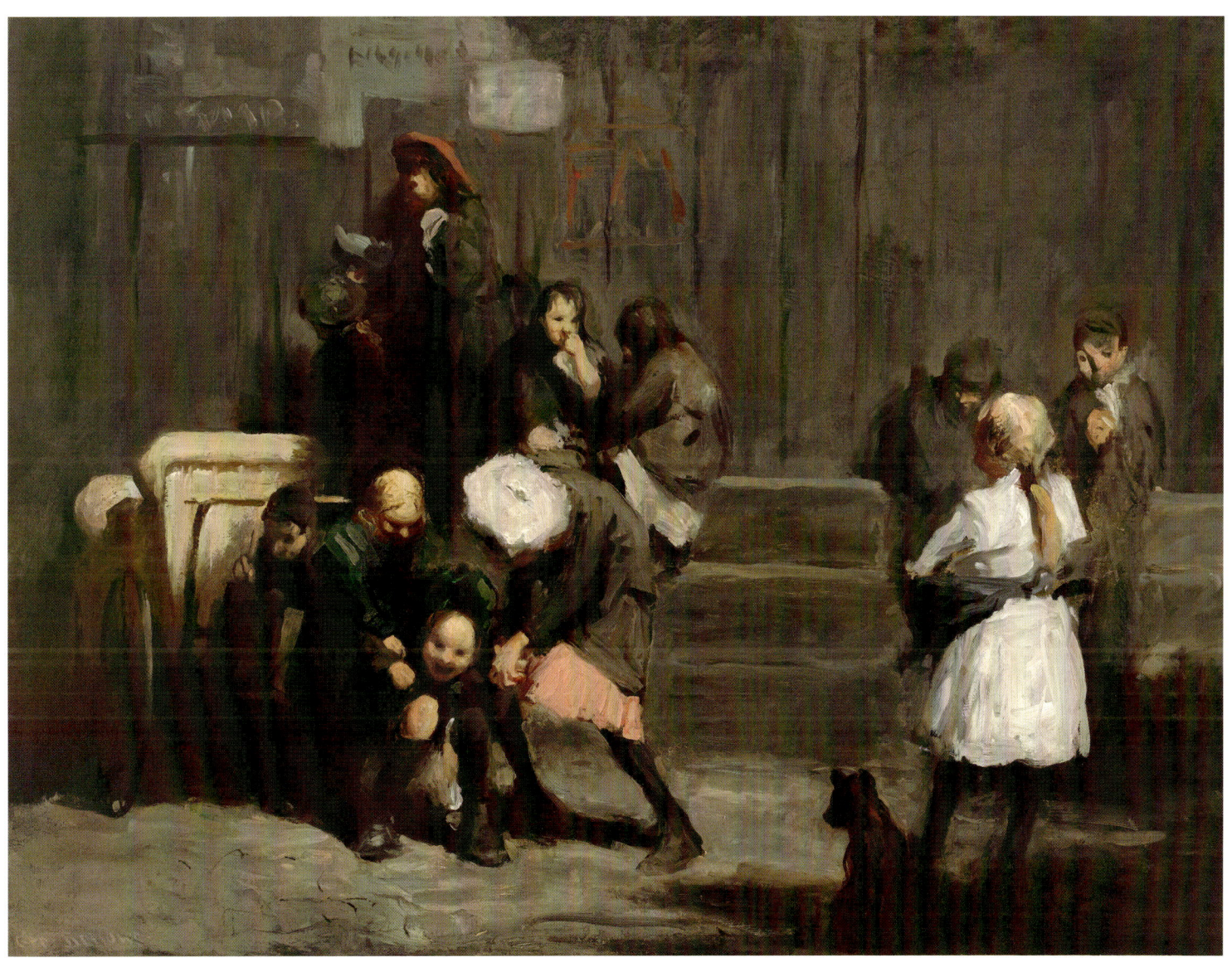

George Bellows (1882–1925), **Kids,** 1906, oil on canvas, 32 x 42 inches

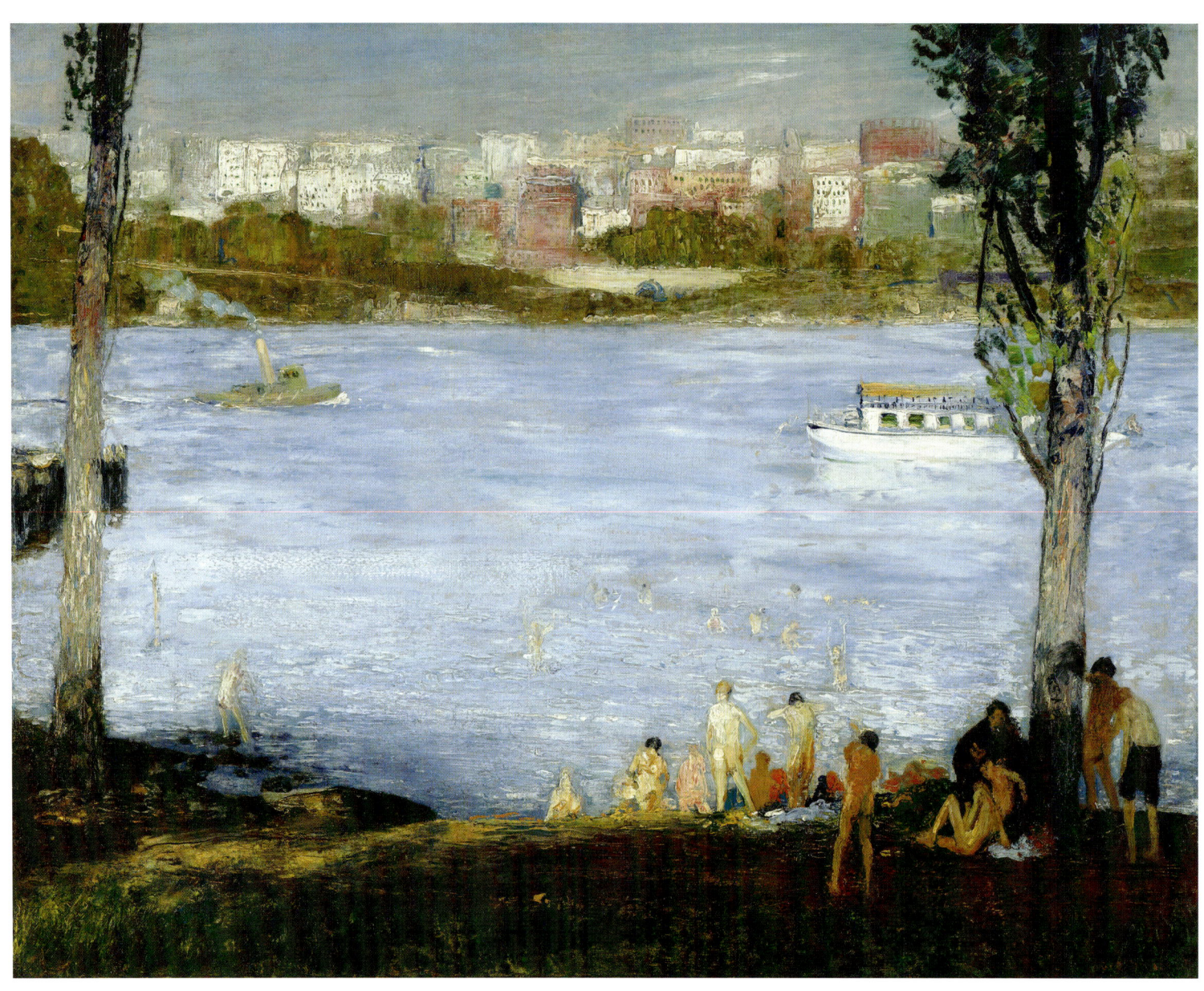

Geⱺrge Bellⱺws (1882–1925), **Summer City,** 1909, oil on canvas, 38 x 48 inches

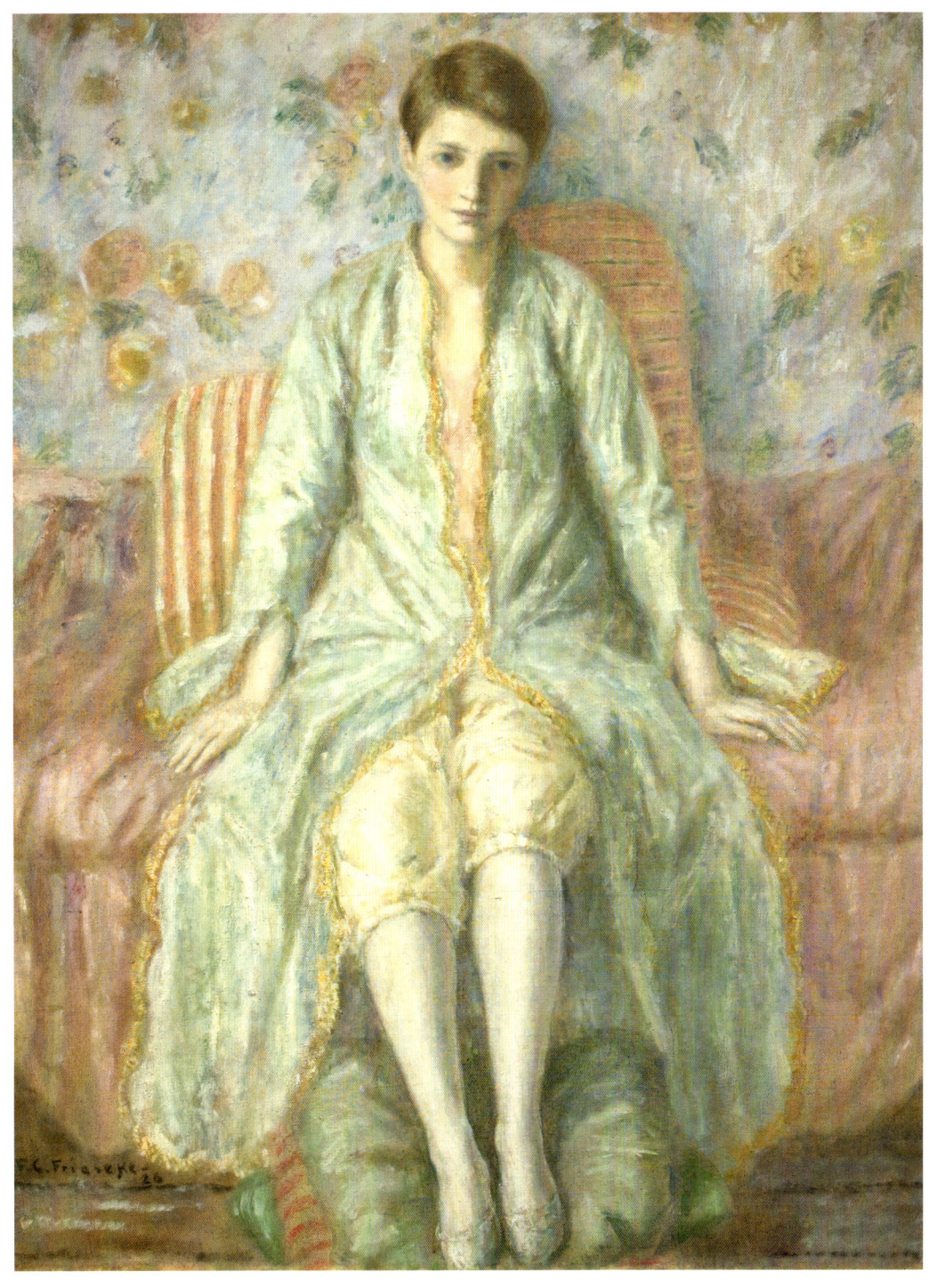

FREDERICK CARL FRIESEKE (1874–1939), **Portrait of Jane Belo,** 1926
Oil on canvas, 52 x 38 inches

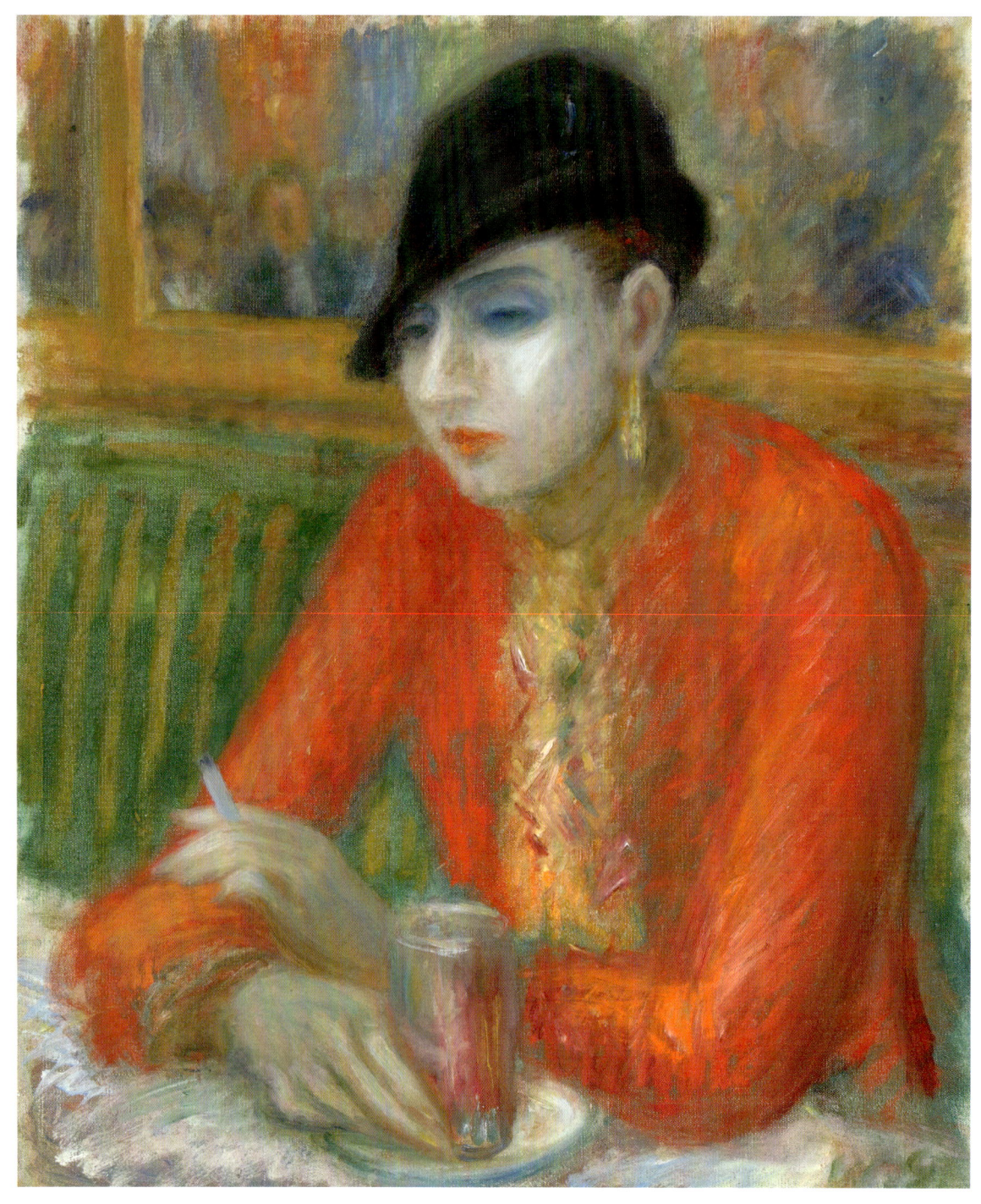

WILLIAM GLACKENS (1870–1938), **L'Aperitif,** 1926, oil on canvas, 18 x 14⅘ inches

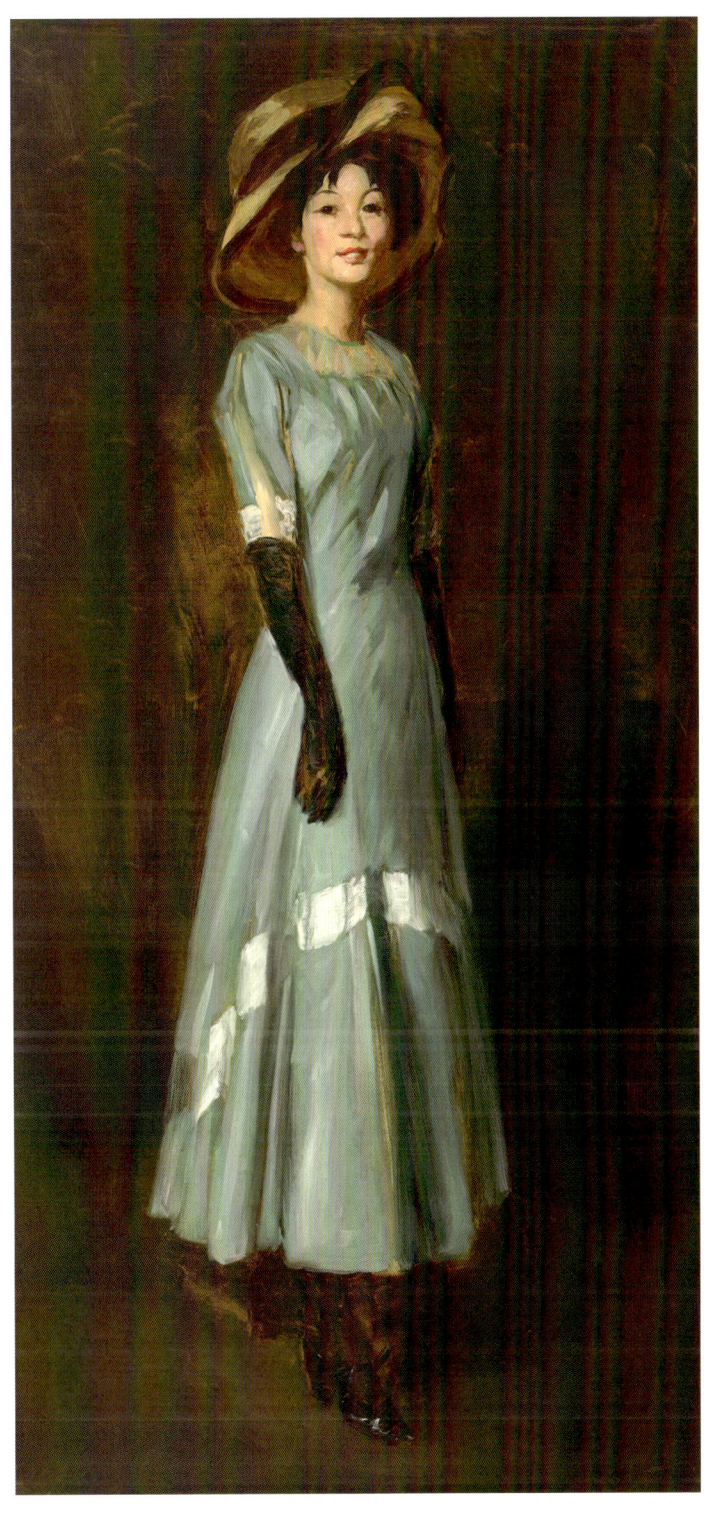

ROBERT HENRI (1865–1929), **Miss Kaji Waki,** 1909
Oil on canvas, 77 x 37 inches

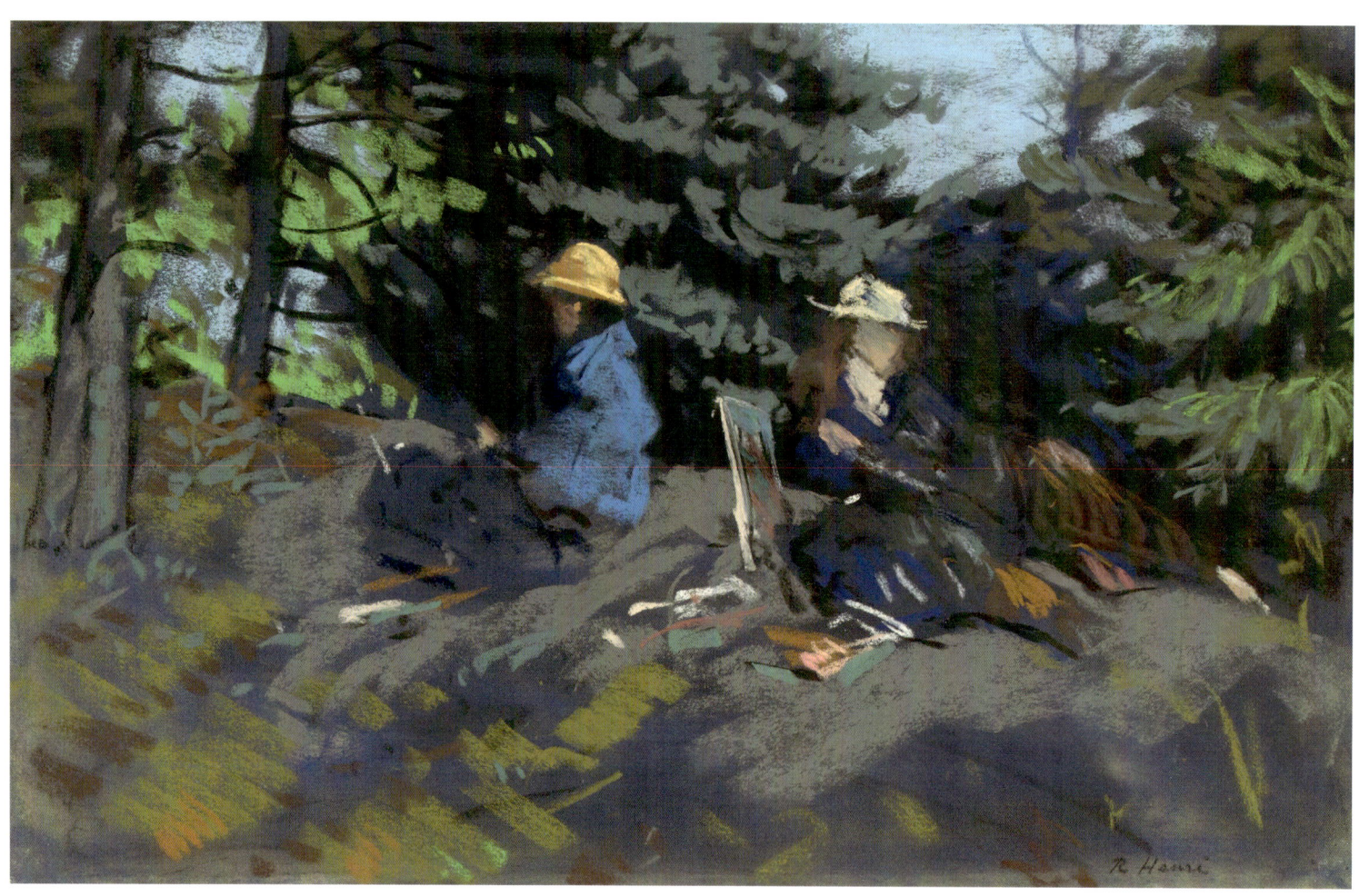

Robert Henri (1865–1929), **The Sketchers,** 1918, pastel on paper, 12⅜ x 19½ inches

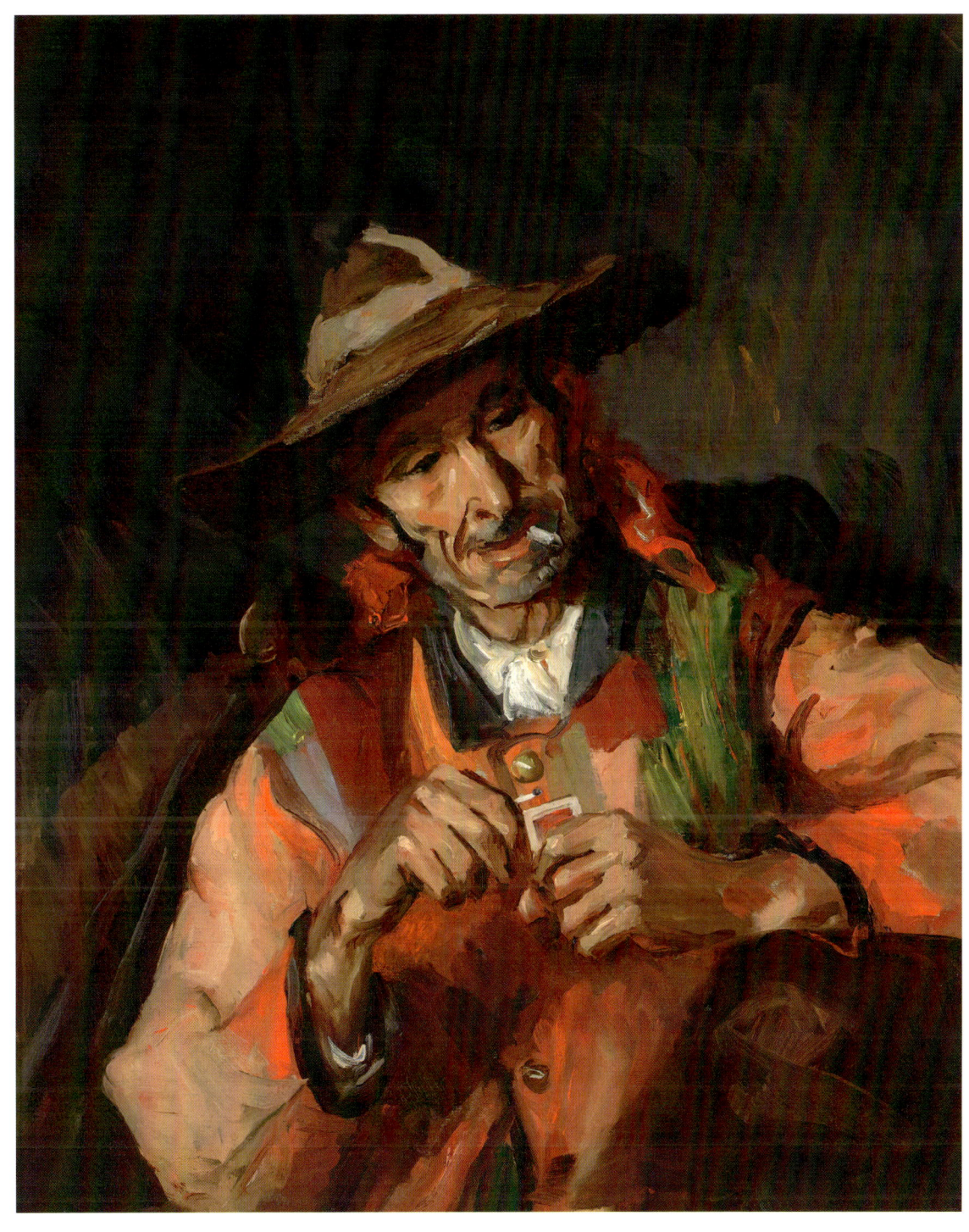

Robert Henri (1865–1929), **Old Spaniard — "Lagartija," Florencio Rodriques,** ca. 1923
Oil on canvas, 32 x 26 inches

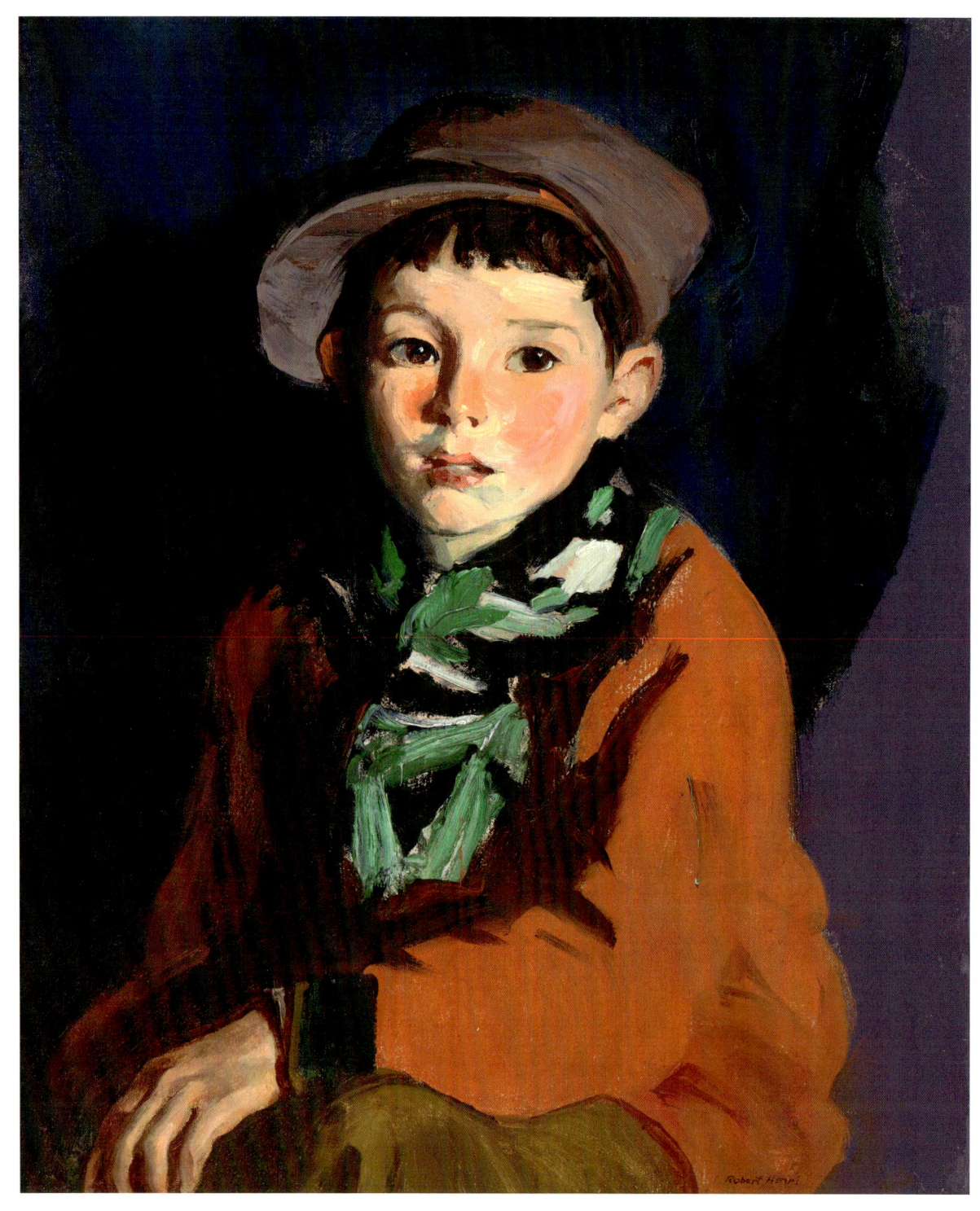

ROBERT HENRI (1865–1929), **Listening Boy,** 1924, oil on canvas, 24 x 20 inches

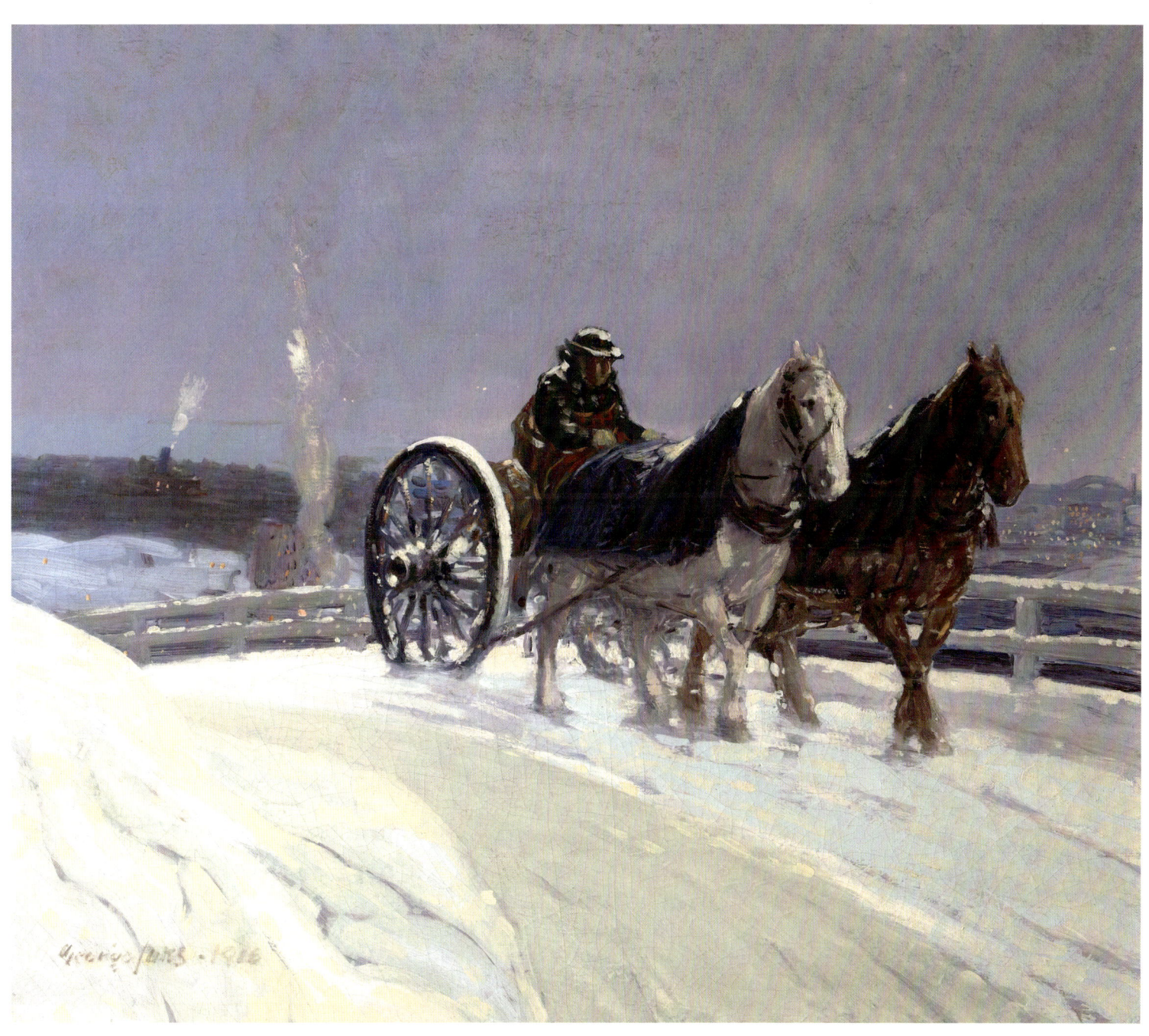

GEORGE LUKS (1867–1933), **The Hitch Team (Horses in the Snow),** 1916, oil on canvas, 39 x 44¾ inches

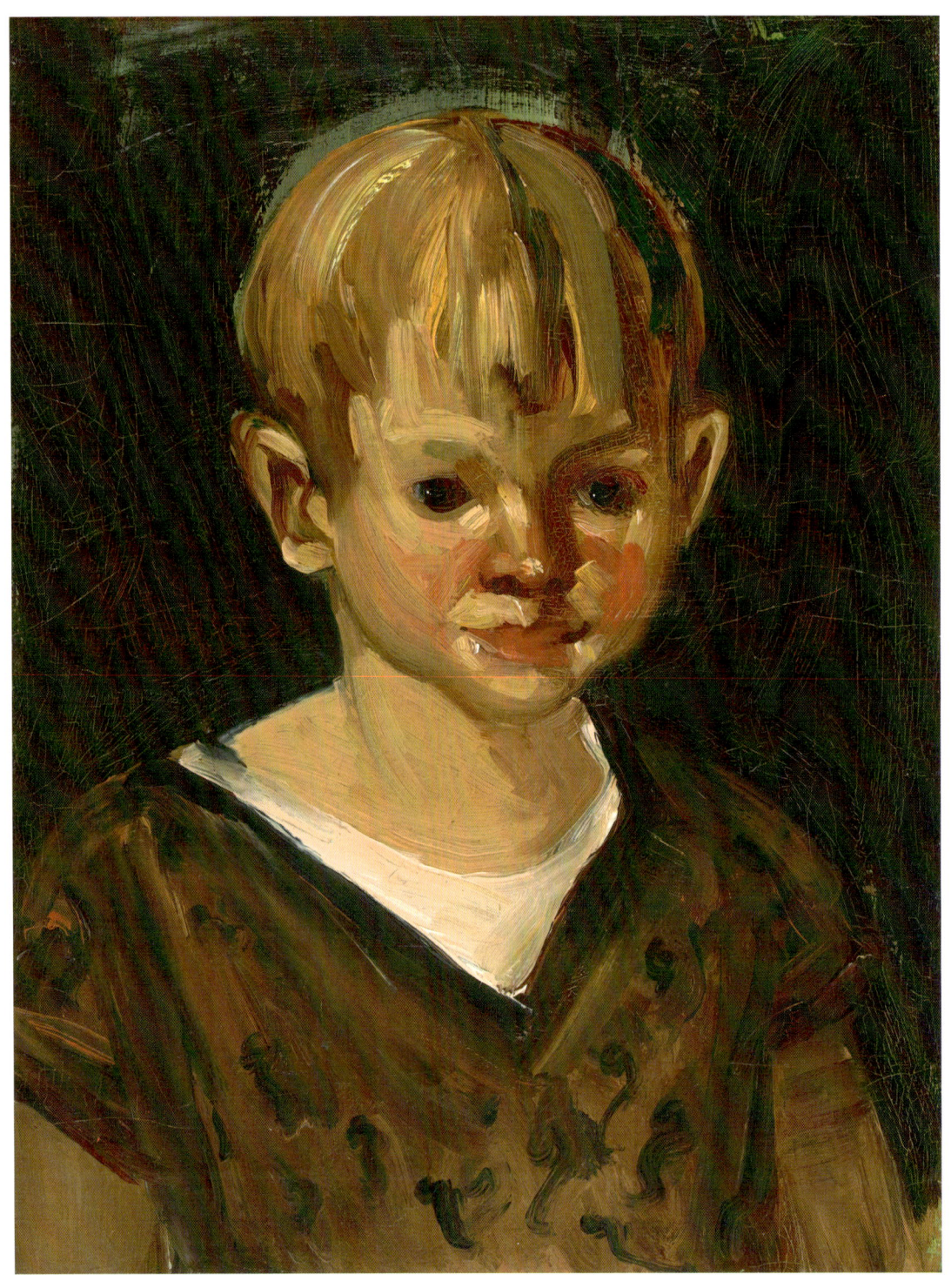

Geore Luks (1867–1933), **Young Boy,** early 1920s, oil on canvas, 16 x 12 inches

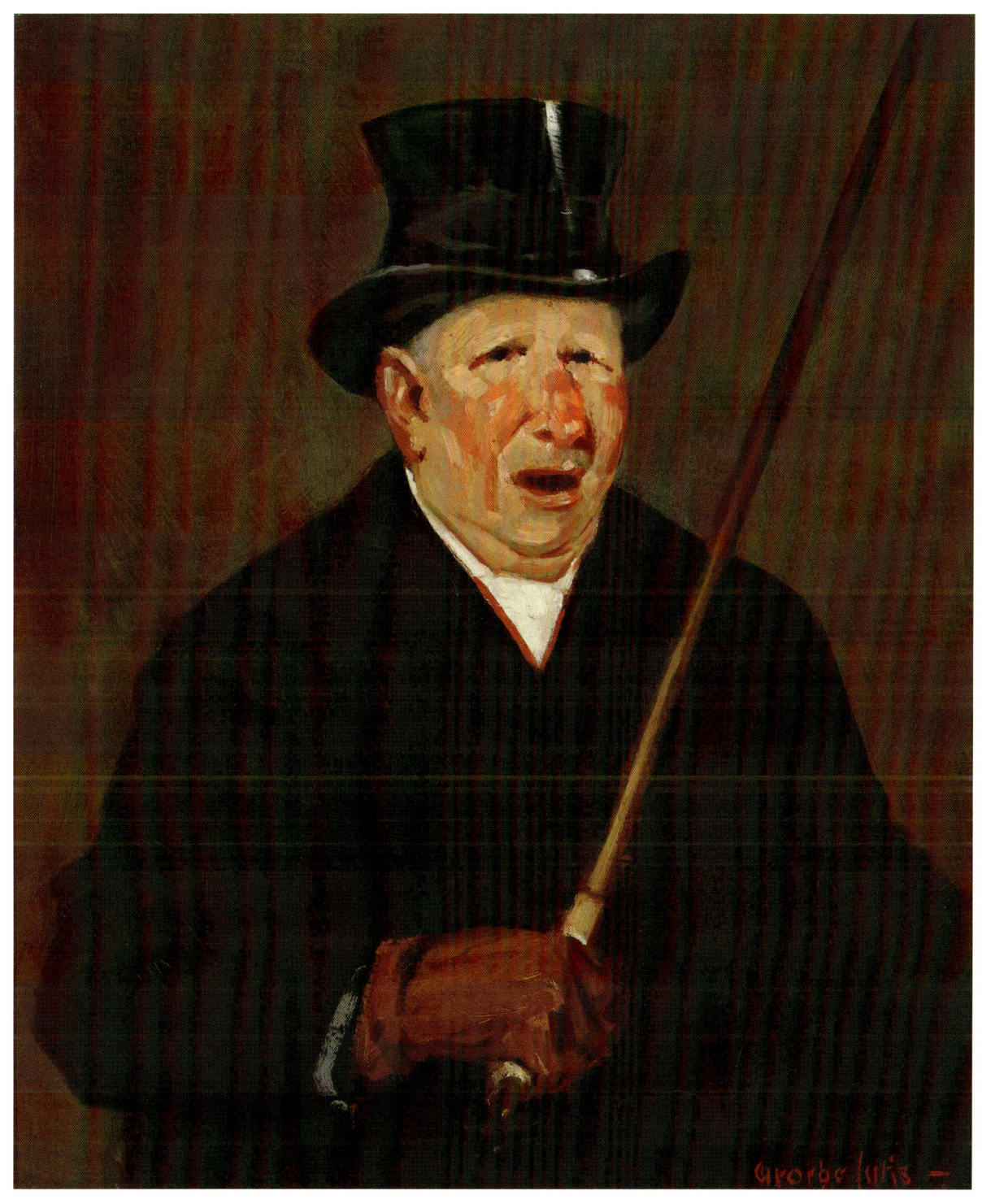

GEORGE LUKS (1867–1933), **The Cabby,** 1921, oil on canvas, 29 ½ x 24 ½ inches

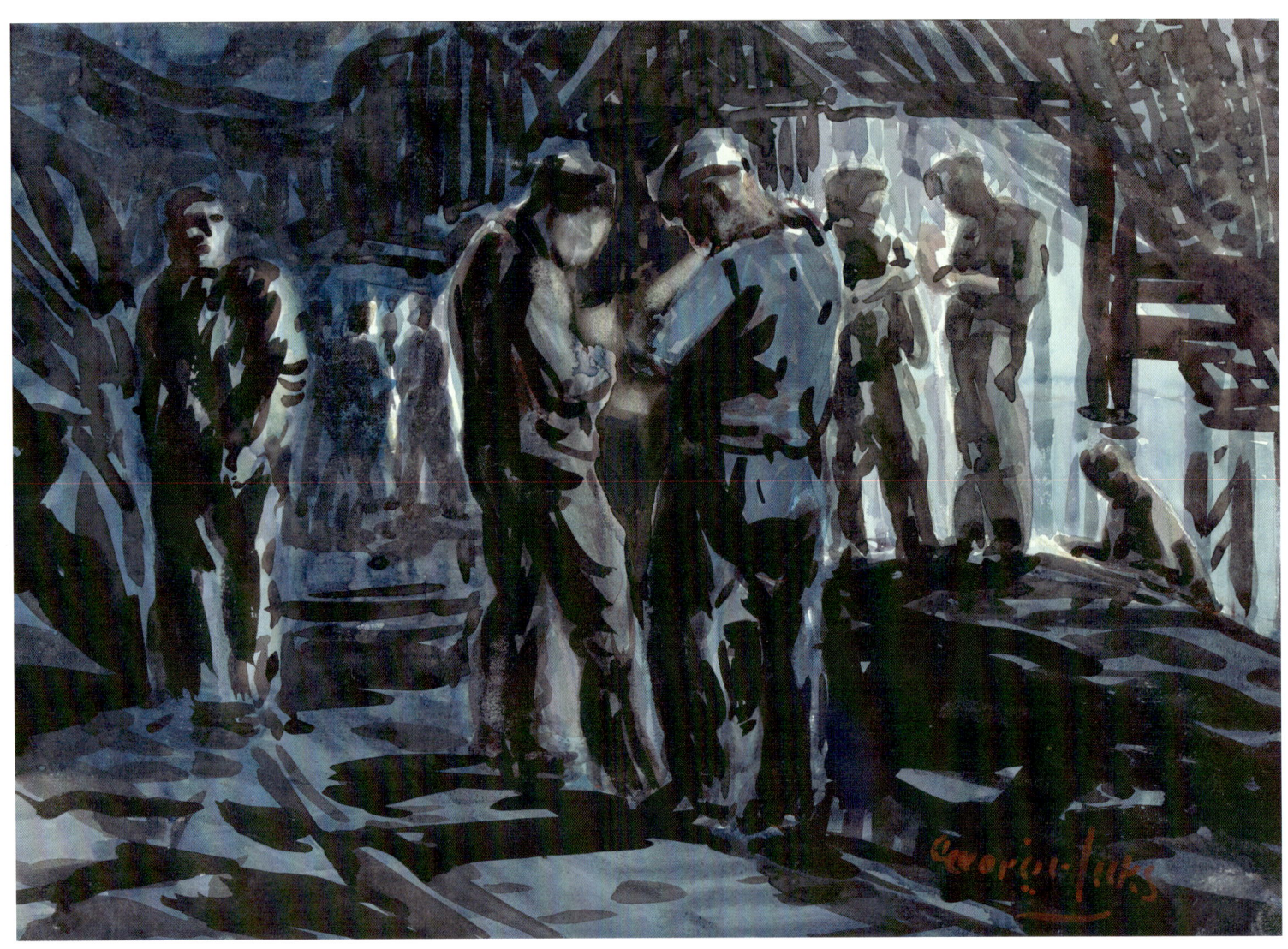

GEORGE LUKS (1867–1933), **Coal Miners,** mid–1920s, gouache on paper laid on board, 14 ³⁄₁₀ x 20 inches

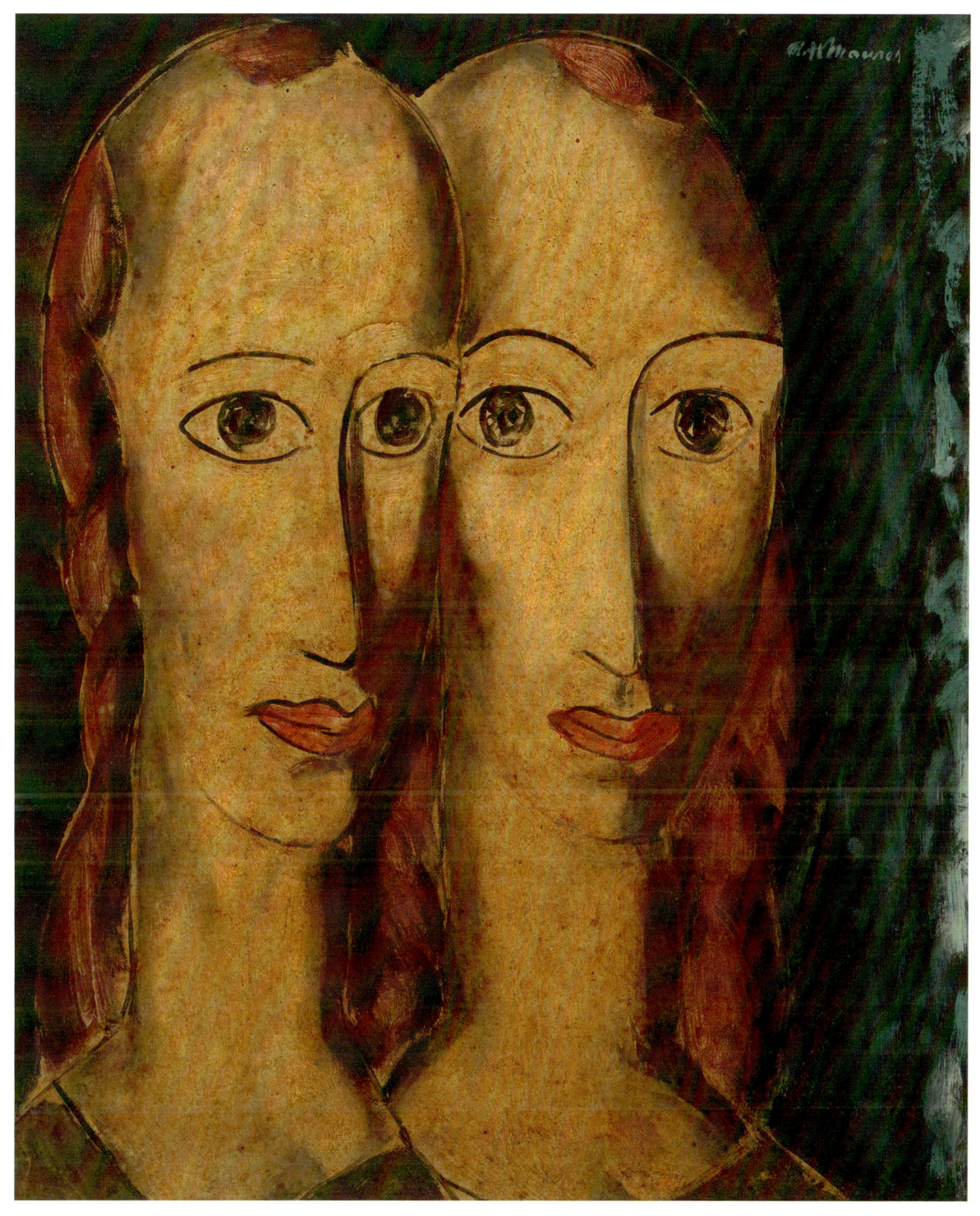

ALFRED MAUER (1868–1932), **Sisters,** ca. 1925, oil on board, 21¾ x 18 inches

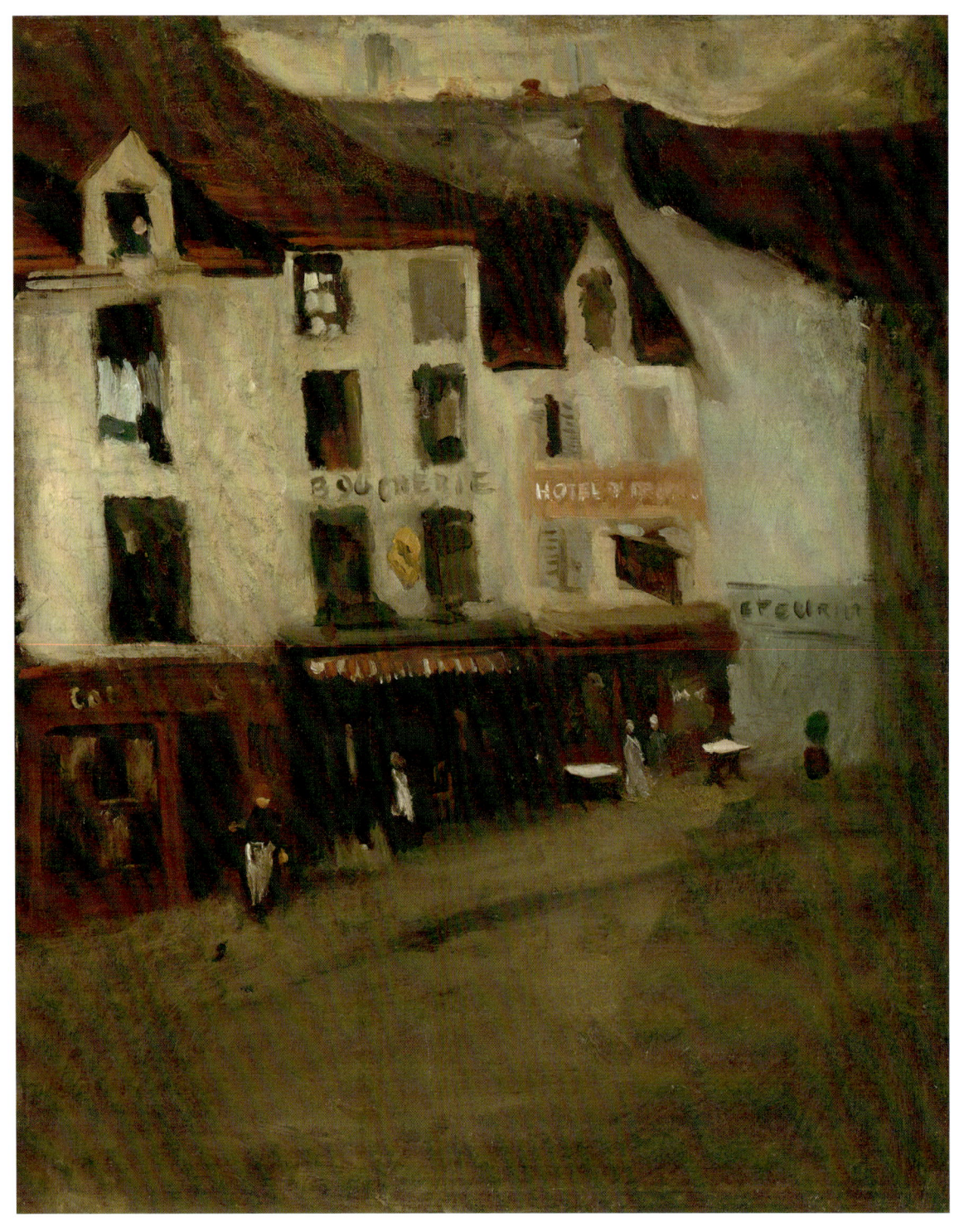

Guy Pène du Bois (1884–1958), **Paris Street,** 1905, oil on canvas, 32 x 25⅘ inches

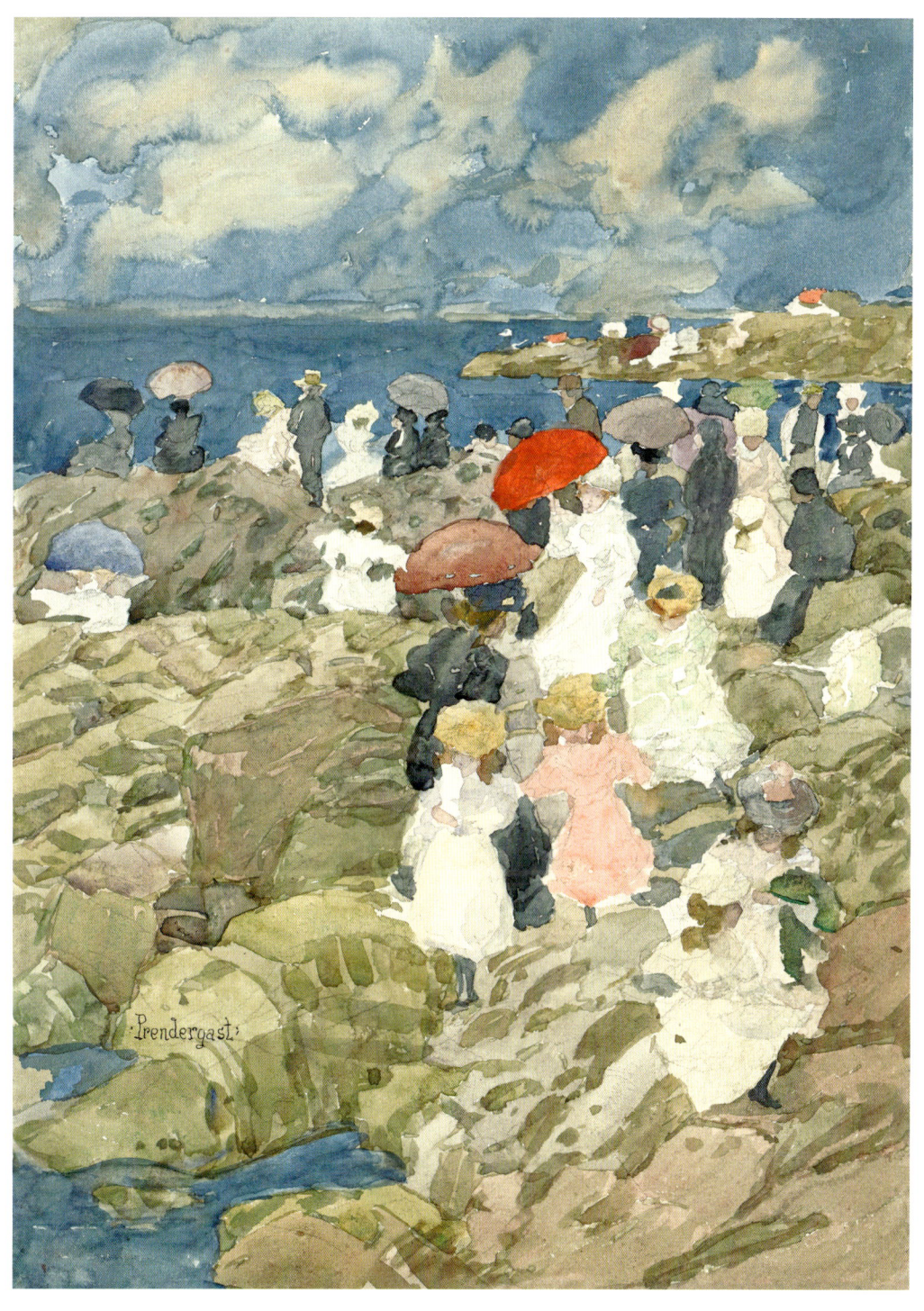

Maurice Prendergast (1858–1924), **Handkerchief Point,** ca. 1896–97
Watercolor over graphite on paper, 13½ x 9⅝ inches

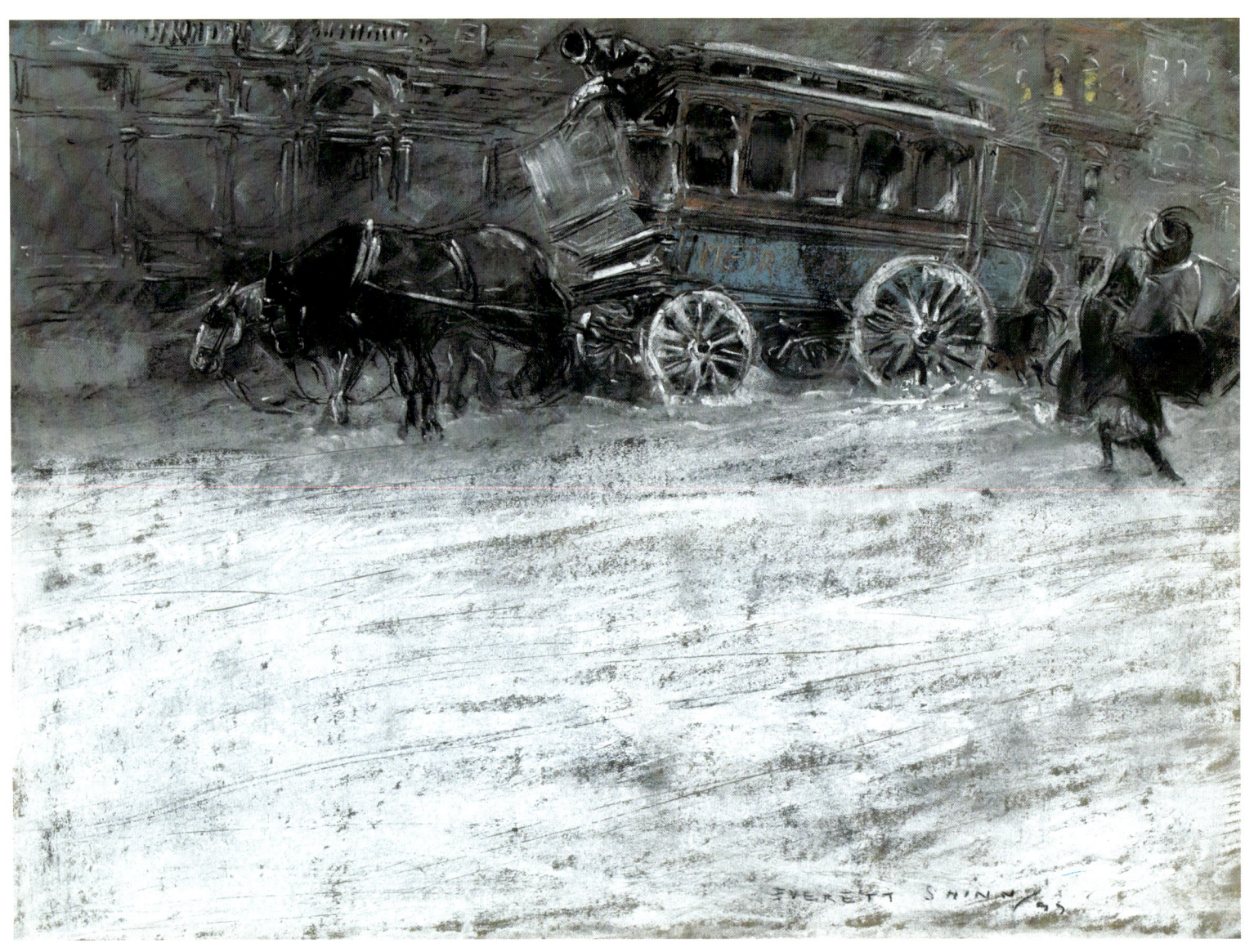

EVERETT SHINN (1876–1953), **Horsedrawn Bus,** 1899, pastel on paper, 21¾ x 29⅝ inches

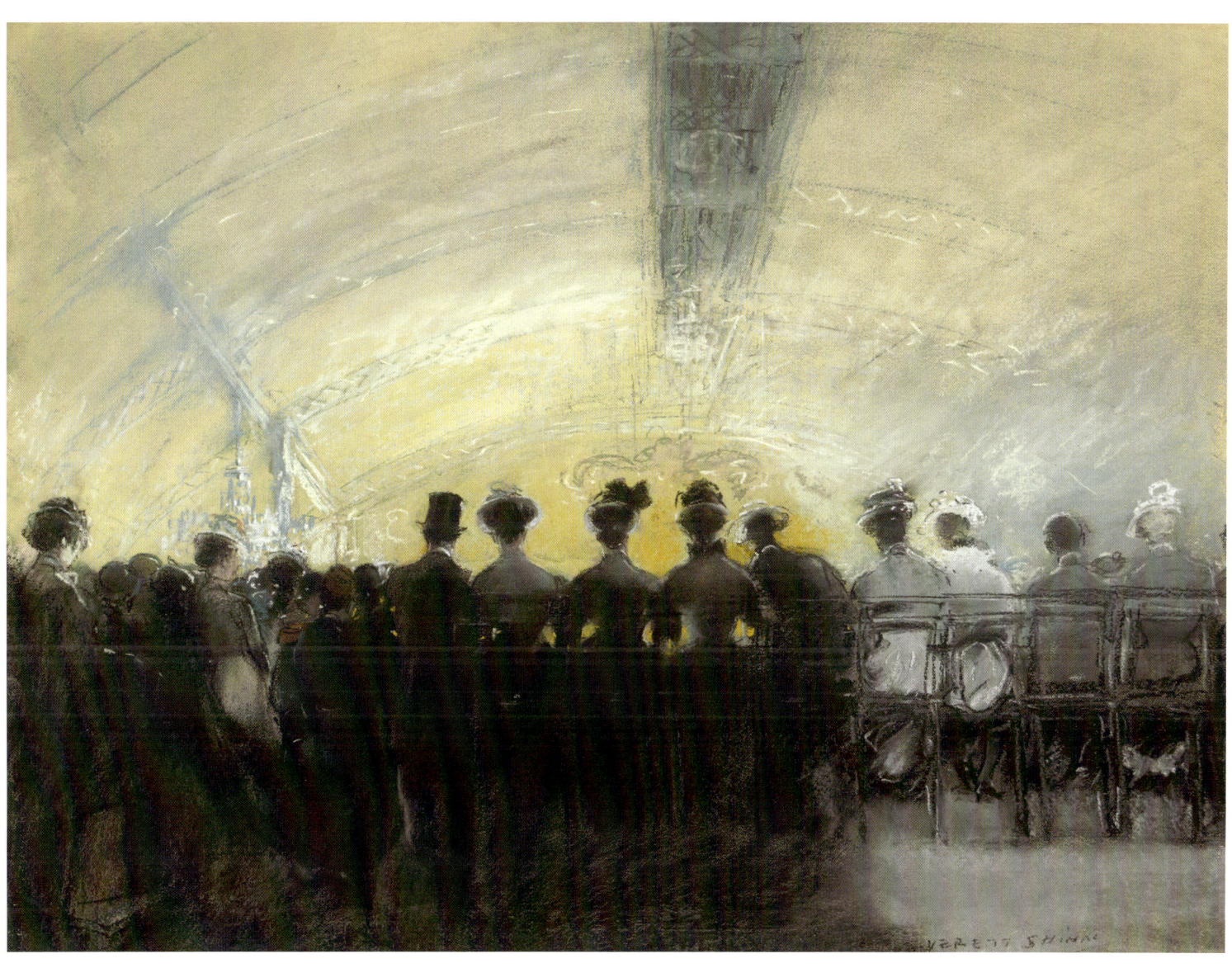

Everett Shinn (1876–1953), **Back Row, Folies-Bergère,** 1900, pastel on paper, 20½ x 27 inches

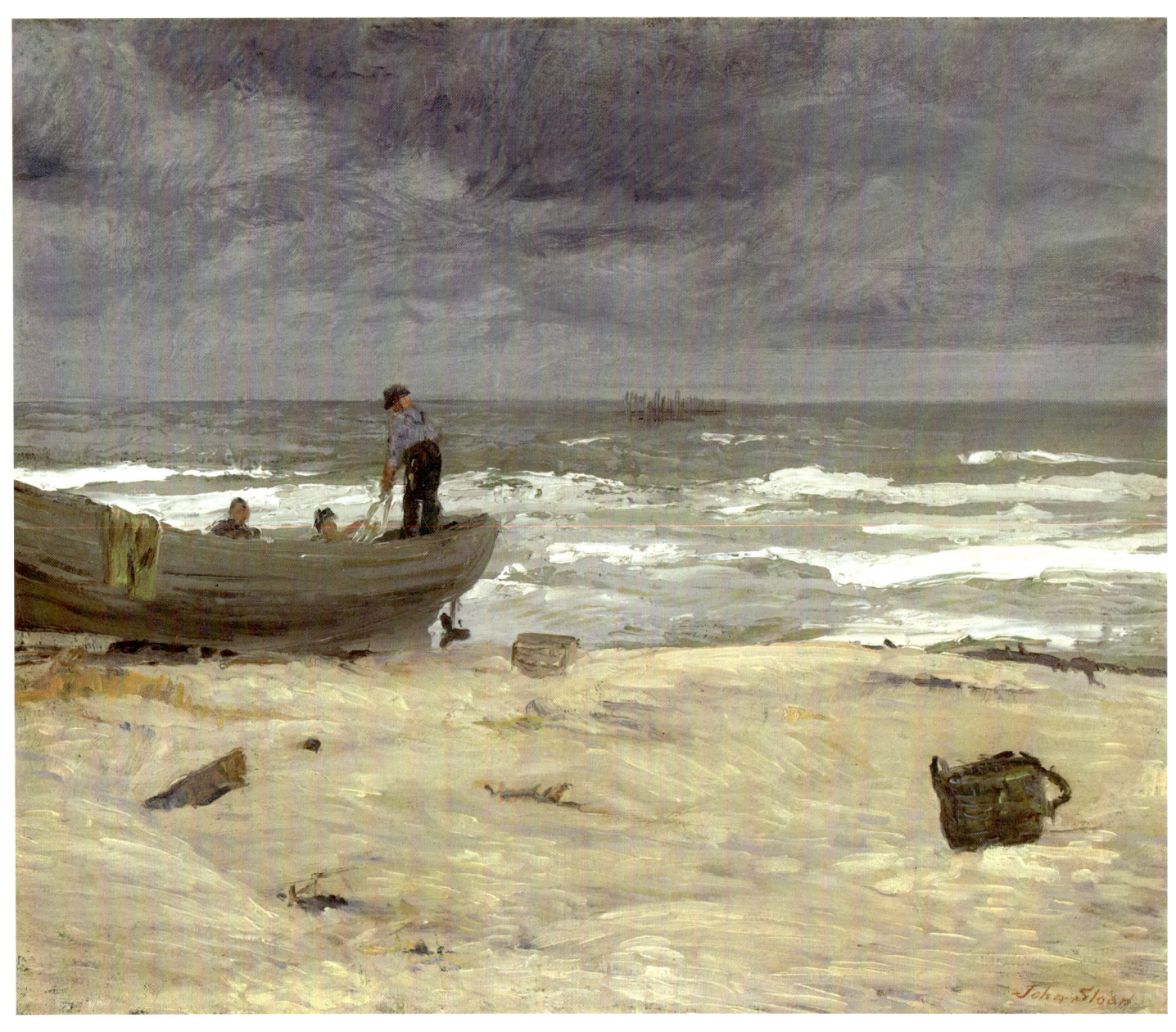

John Sloan (1871–1951), **Gray Day, Jersey Coast,** 1911, oil on canvas, 22 x 26 ¼ inches

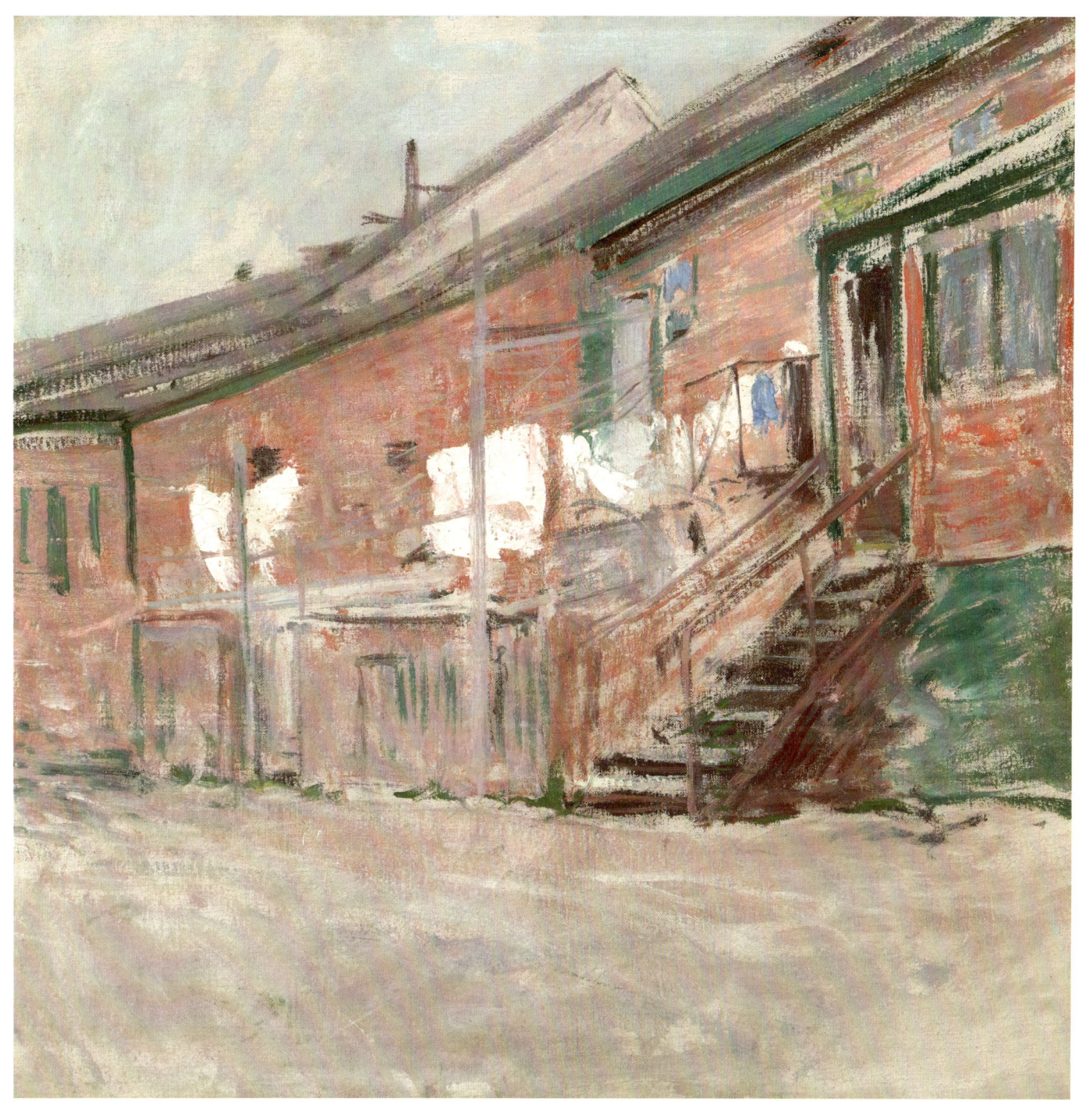

John Twachtman (1853–1902), **Gloucester, Fishermen's Houses,** ca. 1900
Oil on canvas, 25 x 25 ½ inches

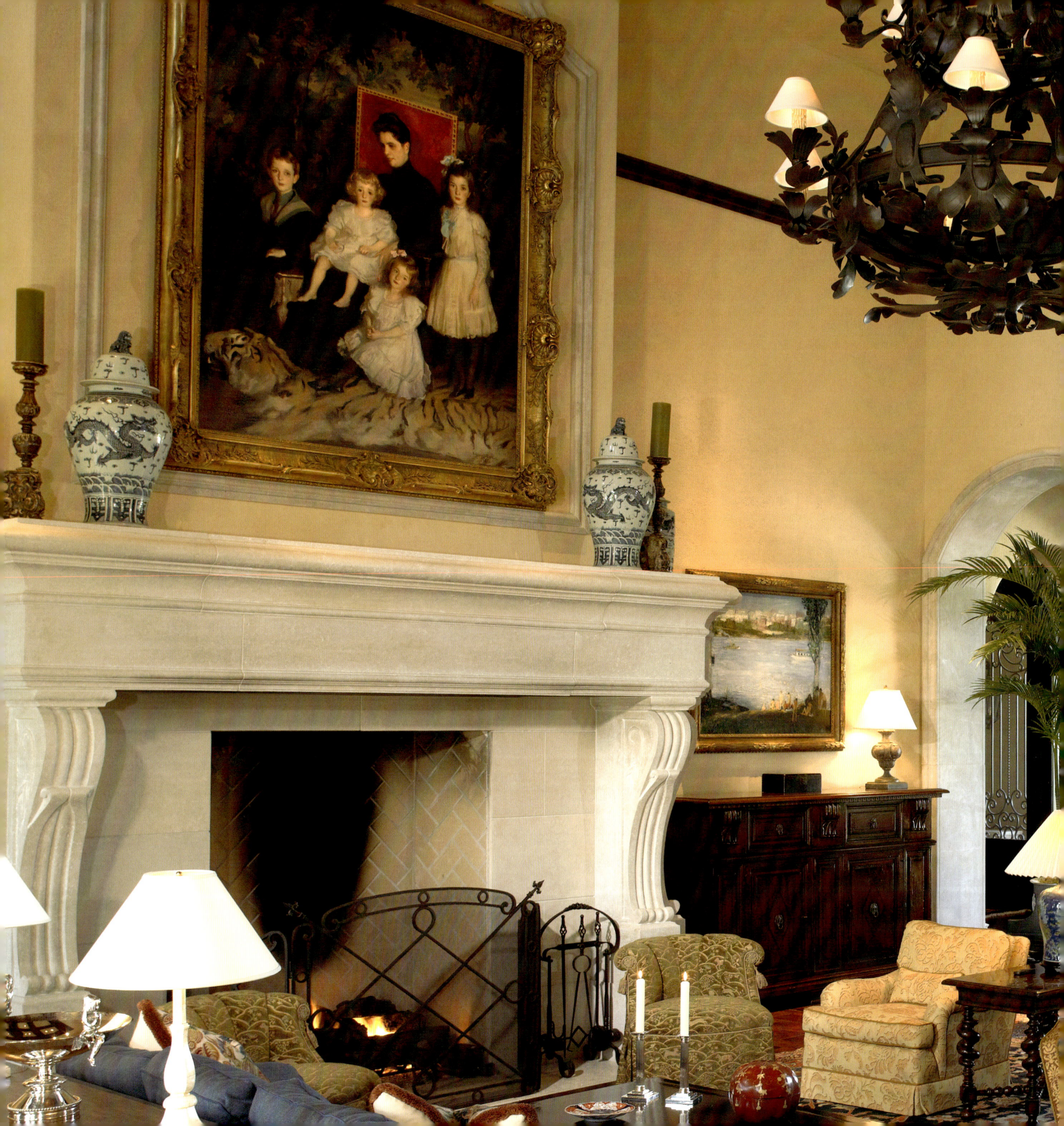

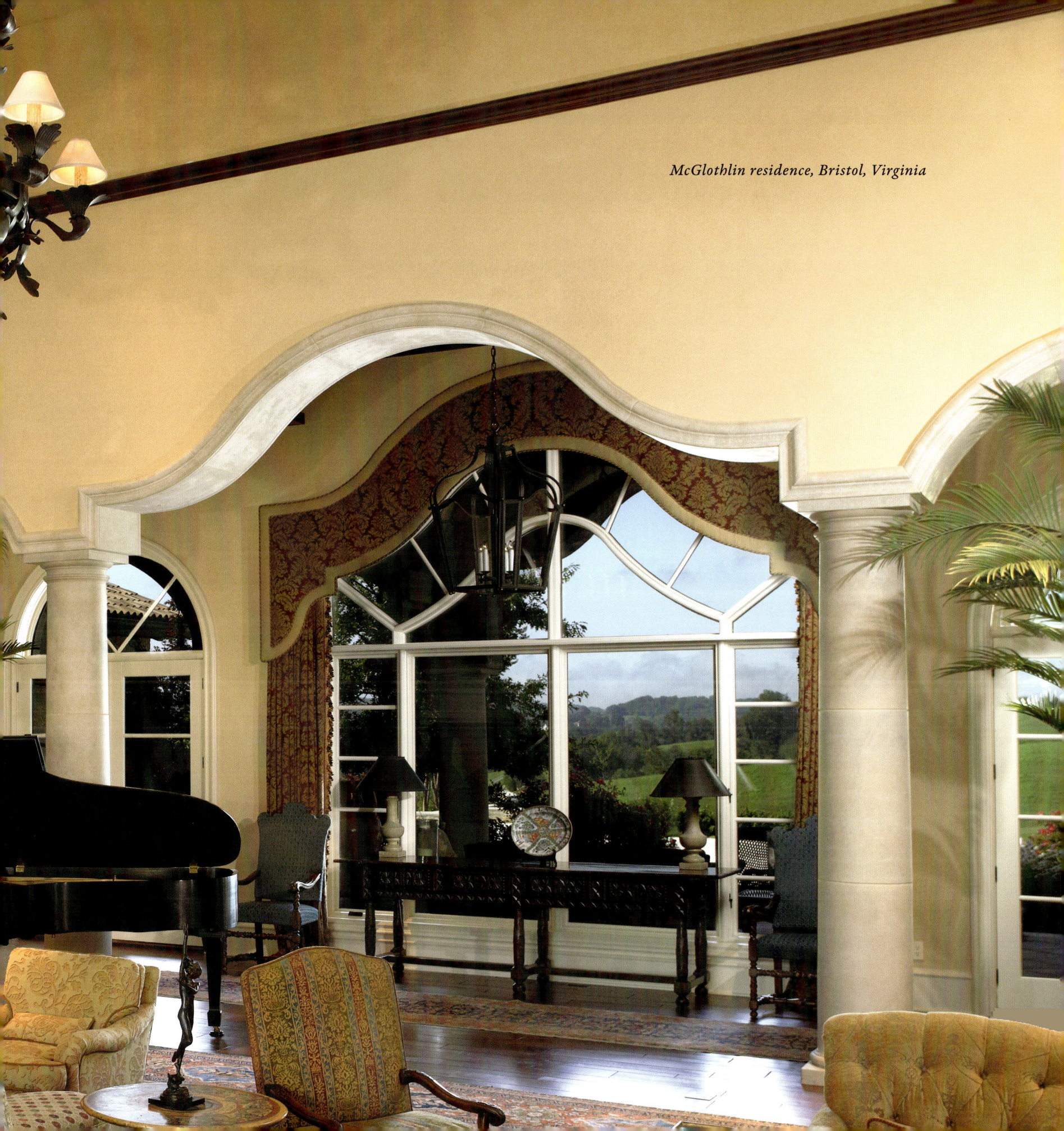

McGlothlin residence, Bristol, Virginia

Index by artist

Index by object